Parenting a Child with a Learning Disability

Also by Cheryl Gerson Tuttle and Penny Paquette

Thinking Games to Play With Your Child

Parenting a Child *with a* Learning Disability

A Practical, Empathetic Guide

Cheryl Gerson Tuttle

Penny Paquette

LOWELL HOUSE
Los Angeles

CONTEMPORARY BOOKS
Chicago

Library of Congress Cataloging-in-Publication Data

Tuttle, Cheryl Gerson.
Parenting a child with a learning disability : a practical, empathetic guide / Cheryl Gerson Tuttle and Penny Paquette.
p. cm.
Includes bibliographical references and index.
ISBN 1-56565-082-4
1. Learning disabled children—Education—United States. 2. Parent and child—United States. 3. Education—United States—Partent participation. 4. Learning disabilities—United States. I. Paquette, Penny Hutchins. II.Title.
LC4705.T87 1993
649'.152—dc20 93-1646
CIP

Publisher: Jack Artenstein
Vice-President/Editor-in-Chief: Janice Gallagher
Director of Publishing Services: Mary D. Aarons
Text design: Nancy Freeborn

Manufactured in the United States of America
10 9 8 7 6 5 4 3 2 1

This book is dedicated to Frances Gerson Siegel—my parental role model, my friend, and my mother.

C.G.T.

For my mother and my sister, who love me and taught me so much about families.

P.P.

Table of Contents

Foreword

As a practicing pediatrician of 30 years, with a particular interest in children with learning disabilities, I welcome a book like this.

Long after learning disabilities were recognized as a cause of school failure and low self-esteem, children were still called lazy, dumb, unmotivated, class clowns, retarded, and behavior problems.

Some of these children, through tremendous willpower and tenacity and with great support from parents and teachers, make it through school and become productive citizens. More often than not, however, they fail in school, drop out, and never acquire the skills necessary to succeed.

Today, fortunately, methods exist to diagnose and treat children with various types of learning disabilities.

This book, written by an experienced team in the field of special education and parenting, addresses the problems of learning disabilities in everyday language that parents can understand and use in order to help their child succeed.

It explains the various types of learning disabilities with concrete examples parents will recognize. The book provides specific suggestions to help parents with many of the situations they will face every day.

It helps them work through feelings of denial, anger, powerlessness, and disappointment following the diagnosis of a learning disability and helps guide them through the acceptance process so they can move on to the business of aiding their child.

Using the suggestions in this book, parents will learn how to support each other and to relate not only to their learning disabled child, but to their other children as well. They will learn to focus their energies and to make the most of each day.

Chapters detail the many types of learning difficulties that exist, including reading, speech, writing, and math, and explain how the disabilities can affect a child's self-esteem. In addition, the authors give many practical suggestions on how to be assertive where the educational rights of children are concerned.

The authors provide a concise and understandable explanation of the different educational tests that may be administered to a child. An extensive glossary defines special educational terms.

The chapters entitled "Adolescence" and "The Team Approach" are superb and should be read very carefully.

Mainly, this book gives hope. If parents use it as a tool, they will learn how to work within the school system for their child's benefit without being overwhelmed by the special educational process. Parents and children will be motivated to persevere and to succeed. With guidance and support, the learning disabled child will develop a renewed sense of self-worth, and with high self-esteem, children have the means to achieve their full potential.

Thank you, Mesdames Tuttle and Paquette, for writing this invaluable book.

Michael K. Levine, M.D.
Atlanta, GA

Acknowledgments

The authors would like to thank the many students, parents, and teachers who agreed to be interviewed. Without their cooperation, there would be no book.

A special debt of gratitude goes to Barbara DeLeo, who got us started.

We would like to especially thank the following educational professionals who recognized our vision for this book and generously shared their experiences: Christine Allen, Teresa Alpert, Candace Barackman, Susan Cullen, Kathleen Dempsey, Susan Egan, Judy Jacobi, Christine Lenahan, Janice Magno, Ruth Melkonian, Kathleen Monahan, Ellen Pierson, Paula Seaver, and Colleen Shaw.

We would also like to thank several psychologists who shared their special understanding of children with learning disabilities, including Tom Kelleher, Diana King, John E. Lappen, Jr., and Carol Lewis.

We thank the National Association of State Directors of Special Education and the Federation for Children with Special Needs for providing resource lists. Thanks also to the National Center for Learning Disabilities for permission to reprint their statement on parent education.

Most of all we would like to thank our families for their support and encouragement, especially Gerald Tuttle for his phenomenal proofreading skills.

Preface

Parent Education

Prepared by the Professional Advisory Board, National Center for Learning Disabilities

NCLD recognizes that parents are the first and most important teachers of their children. The family is the chief socializing agent in the child's life; it is in the family that the child develops, or fails to develop, a sense of safety and belonging. It is here that children learn from parents and siblings the value of becoming contributing, productive members of the larger society.

Parents of children with learning disabilities share all the responsibilities of parenthood and in addition they often feel isolated and inadequate. We believe that these parents should be supported in their efforts to become effective advocates for their children within the family as well as within the schools and the community.

No one knows a child better than his parents. Children who know that their parents are strong advocates for them have a basis for developing a sense of competency and self-esteem.

The successful parenting of a learning disabled child first involves learning what LD is and what it is not.

- Learning disabilities manifest themselves in many ways and produce recognizable behaviors.
- Children with LD are found in every class, race, and ethnic group.

- Neither the parent nor the child is to blame for the disability.

Parents need help in grasping and accepting the nature of the child's difficulties in learning. They need support for the long haul of working with and for their child. Parent support groups, conferences, and books and periodicals can help parents through this process. One of the most important things parents can do is to become partners in their child's education and to work cooperatively with school personnel.

There are no easy answers. Being a parent of a learning disabled child is a time-consuming job. It requires investigating alternative learning methods, developing advocacy skills, and learning to observe, to listen, and to know when to intervene. Parents who have an open and flexible approach to problem-solving usually find the process less difficult.

When a child has a learning disability, the entire family is affected. Non-LD siblings and relatives may need help in understanding and accepting the special treatment the LD child receives. This may create additional problems for the parents, who may be accused of playing favorites, or who may find that coping with the learning disability saps their own feelings of worth.

Parents may help their LD child and other family members by emphasizing the LD child's strengths. Often LD children have special gifts in art, music, drama, athletics, or in a particular academic area.

In cooperation with other national organizations, NCLD is committed to fostering parent awareness of LD. Awareness includes these factors:

- Differentiating between learning disabilities and other causes of academic and social problems.
- Knowledge of the rights of the learning disabled as specified in federal and state laws.
- Access to resources for information, for diagnosis, and for treatment of learning disabilities.

The National Center for Learning Disabilities believes that, as the child's primary teacher, the parent should be aided to the fullest extent in providing effectively for the learning disabled child.

The National Center for Learning Disabilities (NCLD) statement is reprinted here with the permission of the NCLD.

Introduction

Kathy Ann walked into her first meeting with her son's special education team. Six specialists greeted her. Before the first one opened her mouth, Kathy Ann felt intimidated. She wasn't prepared for this.

They began by telling her that her son's psychoeducational evaluation identified a discrepancy between his cognitive ability and his academic achievement. "He needs help in the areas of visual processing, sensory integration, and motor planning," they said.

Kathy Ann tried to absorb what they were telling her, but what she wanted to say was, "What in the world are you talking about?" Like most parents new to the special education system, she didn't have a clue. And it wasn't because she was uneducated or unintelligent. She was simply overwhelmed by their language.

The terms are enough to boggle the mind—ADD, ADHD, CST, dyslexia, dyscalculia, dysgraphia, IEP, PPVT, SI, SST. Well-intentioned professionals often use terms that are intimidating to those seeking information on learning problems. Parents sometimes feel they need a dictionary or Physician's Desk Reference just to understand what specialists are saying about their child. Penny and I hope to take some of the mystery out of the subject and offer a clear introduction for parents of children with learning disabilities.

Parenting a Child with a Learning Disability was written to help you understand your child's special learning needs. It is not a medical text or the final professional word on any specific learning disability. It was written to help you, the parent, understand your child's learning disability and to help you cope with the emotional situations that often arise in families affected by learning disability.

When parents find out that their child has a learning disability, it is important for them to realize that when they combine energies with specialists in the field, they can help their child become a successful student and a valuable member of society. Many parents and children have been through the learning disabilities maze and have survived—many have flourished. You and your child can too.

The book reviews the major areas of learning disability. It provides information on what to look for in your child's school, and it gives an overview of the special education laws and your child's rights under the law. Penny and I explain how to work with your child's teacher and with the schools to ensure your child gets the best education he or she can, and we will tell you what to do if you believe the schools are failing your child.

We have consulted the true "experts" in the field of parenting a child with learning disabilities. These experts started where you are right now. They are parents of children with learning disabilities. Some are in the early stages of their child's educational experience, while many others have survived the process to see their child off to college or into the work place. They can help you understand those feelings of guilt and fear and why your home life has become so stressful. They have been through the emotions, the evaluations, the individualized educational plans, and the ups and downs of parenting a child with a learning disability. They share proven, practical advice to help guide you through the process.

So get ready. It's sometimes a rocky road, but often it is a most exciting and stimulating ride!

Chapter 1

Learning Disabilities—What They Are, What They're Not

To begin a discussion of learning disabilities, it is important to know the difference between learning styles (particular strengths and weaknesses) and learning disabilities.

All of us have a particular learning style, whether we recognize it or not. As adults, we unconsciously know how we best absorb information, and we use that method whenever possible. Some adults never write anything down, yet they remember what needs to be done or which items they need at the grocery store. I can't remember all the tasks I need to complete unless I write them down, so I keep a list of projects that need my attention. I don't consider myself to have a disability in the area of memory, but my learning style is such that I need a visual reminder. Most people make these types of adjustments without even thinking about it.

There are three main avenues for learning: hearing, seeing, and doing. Most of us can recognize our learning style by thinking about how we react in a social situation: being introduced to other guests at a party. Those with strong auditory skills will remember names but may not remember faces. Those who are stronger in the visual area might remember faces but forget names. Visual learners might remember a face they have seen only once and retain the memory for a long time. Yet, if you ask them to tell you the name of someone they just met, they often go blank. Those who learn by doing are called kinesthetic learners. They remember the guests' names best by actually writing them down. If they were responsible for making up the guest list, they can recall the names of most of the people at the party.

Think about it. Though most of us use a combination of learning styles, we have strengths in certain areas. We instinctively do what we need to do to avoid our areas of weakness. If we are strong visual or kinesthetic learners, we probably make lists for everything. If there is something we need to remember, we read it several times or practice a task until we accomplish it. If we are stronger in the auditory areas, we might repeat information over and over to ourselves until it is firmly installed in our memory.

Children also have specific learning styles, but most are not mature enough to recognize them. Adults seldom take this fact into consideration when presenting information to children. Children are expected to absorb information no matter how it is presented and to remember it well enough to answer questions about it. Some children can do that, but many can't. And those who can't do not necessarily have learning disabilities.

Learning styles must be taken into consideration when children are expected to learn. In the earliest school years—preschool, kindergarten, first grade—most information is presented orally, in writing, and with hands-on materials children can manipulate. Children are stimulated in all three areas and can learn through the style that is best for them. As children advance in school, however, most schools present the majority of class information orally. This is usually when learning difficulties or learning styles make themselves obvious.

By high school, lectures and class discussions are common. This approach is perfect for those who learn best through hearing information. They may remember what they hear without ever taking a note. Other students need to reinforce what they hear by writing it down and then reading it. Children with strengths in the visual area can reinforce class work with their reading assignments, and they love it when material is presented on film. They will probably remember what they see. For children who learn best by doing, they remember best by writing information down. They can capitalize on their areas of strength in science labs, physical education classes, or technology classes. They might have difficulty learning a science assignment through lectures or readings, but give them the opportunity to mix those chemicals, and the most difficult information begins to make sense.

By high school, most children have learned to compensate for their weaknesses by giving themselves reinforcement in their areas of strength. Visual learners read their notes when they study. Auditory learners repeat their assignments out loud. Kinesthetic learners write the information when they study. The fact that these students have weaknesses does not mean they have learning disabilities. They have learning styles, and they learn to compensate for their weak spots with little or no difficulty.

Those with learning disabilities also have strengths and weaknesses. Children with learning disabilities must be taught how to compensate for their areas of weakness in order to cope with a traditional classroom and social situations. Compensation skills do not come naturally for these children. Learning disabled children are not mentally retarded or impaired, and they certainly shouldn't be called stupid. In fact, most learning disabled children have normal or higher intelligence, and many are gifted. They just have trouble learning to read, write, speak, or compute math.

According to the National Center for Learning Disabilities (NCLD), between 10 and 15 percent of the U. S. population has some form of learning disability. The problem is complex.

Researchers continue to search for explanations, but as yet there is no concrete identifiable cause for learning disabilities.

Many believe the origin is neurological. The brain somehow short-circuits so that information cannot flow in a normal pattern. Some researchers suggest these brain abnormalities can be measured with an electroencephalogram (EEG). Many students with learning disabilities show no indication of brain dysfunction, however.

Some evidence suggests that learning disabilities may have a hereditary, genetic component. Recent studies of twins indicate that when one twin has a reading disability, the identical twin is more likely to suffer the same disability than when the twins are fraternal (nonidentical). Much of our anecdotal research indicates a strong correlation between parents with learning disabilities and children with similar problems. Still, many families of learning disabled children have no history of learning problems.

Environmental factors such as maternal drug and alcohol use during pregnancy may be a contributor. Lead poisoning, inadequate nutrition, and low birth weight may play a role. Specialists still are not sure.

Just as the causes for learning disabilities are unclear, definitions can also be vague. Because much of this book deals with relationships among children, schools, and special education laws, we will use the federal definition for our purposes:

"Specific learning disability means a disorder in one or more of the basic psychological processes involved in understanding or in using language, spoken or written, which may manifest itself in an imperfect ability to listen, think, speak, read, write, spell, or to do mathematical calculations..."

Or, as the NCLD says, "Learning disabilities create a gap between a person's true capacity and his or her day-to-day productivity and performance."

There is no typical profile of a learning disabled child and no one thing you can point to with confidence and say, "Aha, that's the problem!"

The most common characteristics of children with learning disabilities are:

- Difficulty with academic skills including reading, writing, speech, and mathematics.
- Difficulty with fine motor skills such as handwriting and copying.
- Difficulty with long- and short-term memory.
- Difficulty with attention (short attention spans, distractability, hyperactivity, impulsivity).
- Difficulty with sensory integration.
- Difficulty with organizational skills.
- Extreme gaps in sections on IQ tests (for example, high verbal scores but poor performance scores).
- Difficulty making and keeping friends.
- Low self-esteem.

Your child may have difficulties in some of these areas yet may not have a learning disability. However, if your child is having problems succeeding in school, you may want to explore the possibility of a learning disability.

Whatever the causes, whatever the characteristics, there certainly is no need to blame yourself for your child's disability, and there is no reason to feel guilty. In my years of teaching I have discovered the cause is not important in working with a child. Each child, whether disabled or not, is unique and needs to be raised and taught with sensitivity to his individuality and his learning style. Though learning disabilities cannot be cured or outgrown, your child can be taught to compensate and can be a successful student.

Though many parents have suspicions about their children's abilities quite early, learning disabilities are usually diagnosed after children enter school. Once a learning disabled child is expected to read, write, or work with numbers, learning problems become obvious. These children need help. Without help, most are doomed to failure in the classroom and often failure in social situations as well. There is help for your child, and she has every right to receive that help. You as the person who knows her best can play a strong role in seeing she receives the help and encouragement she needs.

Chapters 7 through 12 provide more detailed information about specific learning disabilities. Your child may be identified with one or more of these. Once you have learned more about your child's specific learning needs, you will be better prepared to work with the other professionals helping your child.

Chapter 2

Dealing with Emotions

Carolyn got a call from her son's classroom teacher, who wanted to talk about Jonathan's progress. Before the teacher said another word, Carolyn knew what was coming. She knew her son was having trouble in school. His report cards were not as good as she thought they should be. His teacher often sent work home to be corrected, and Jonathan couldn't tell what he had done wrong. Homework sessions were nightmares. She knew he was having difficulty outside of the classroom too. She had watched him play games with children his age. They had no trouble reading the directions, but Jonathan wouldn't even try. She suspected he might have a learning disability, and she was sure that was the reason for the teacher's call.

Yet when Jonathan's teacher said she thought the boy's lack of progress might be caused by a learning disability, Carolyn's reaction surprised her. Though she knew in her heart that her son needed help, she heard herself say, "He doesn't need to be evaluated. He doesn't have a learning disability. Do you have some quota you need to fill? Forget it. He's just immature. He'll outgrow this problem."

Carolyn's reaction was not unusual. When parents have their initial conversation about the possibility of a learning disability, their reactions fall into several categories. Many deny the problem. Others are fearful, some blame themselves, and some are actually relieved. Seldom are they surprised. All the parents we spoke to said they suspected their child had a learning disability long before they received a confirmation from the schools.

Like many parents we spoke to, Carolyn went through a state of denial. Despite the fact that her heart told her her son needed help, she couldn't face a diagnosis of a learning disability. Carolyn's memories prevented her from accepting the facts. Many parents of students with learning disabilities share Carolyn's history. Though she knew little about today's programs, she had no difficulty remembering her own days in a "special" classroom. Carolyn spent many of her school years in the "dummy class." Of course, no teacher ever called it that, but many of the other children at the school did. Even though her classroom was in the basement, away from the "normal" children, Carolyn heard what they said. She didn't want her son burdened by the sad memories she had stored for so long. She didn't want him labeled and treated differently. It was easier to deny her son had a problem.

Parents who have not suffered themselves also find ways to deny the problem.

"He's just lazy."

"She could do fine if she would just listen."

"He's just like his father, and his father did okay in school."

Most mothers Penny and I spoke to said they eventually came to accept the diagnosis in a positive way. The diagnosis meant their child would receive the help he or she needed to succeed.

Fathers often have a more difficult time. Dads seem to have an especially hard time recognizing that learning disabilities can affect both performance and behavior. They are less likely to see the benefits of having their child's program altered to accommodate a learning disability. If their child's educational plans need to be modified, they must acknowledge that their child has special needs. In order to accept a change in their son's or daughter's academic program, they must accept the fact that the child needs more help than a typical student. According to parents and professionals, fathers find it difficult to accept this, for a variety of reasons.

Even though times have changed, fathers in general still have less of a connection with the school than do mothers. They have had less opportunity to develop a relationship with their child's teachers. They often hear about their child's problems from their wives. Seldom are they directly involved in working with the schools. In any case, what fathers want is a child who is 100 percent "normal."

For many of the families we spoke to, the father's denial had to be treated before the child could receive help. Once both parents were committed as advocates for their child, everyone benefited.

Most parents we spoke to said they were angry when they learned their child had a learning disability. They remembered their initial responses:

"Johnny doesn't need special help. What he needs is a better classroom teacher. She doesn't spend enough time with him!"

Or, "I'm fed up with the whole system. How can they say my child has difficulty learning? Isn't that why I'm sending her to school—to learn?"

Or, "These educators just can't get their acts together enough to help my child. They're the ones who need some motivation!" Some parents find it easier to blame the teachers than to accept the fact that their child has a problem.

Many of the parents we spoke to remembered being angry with the teacher, angry with the system, angry with their child's peers, angry with "the gods." They were just plain mad. And often that led to another reaction: guilt.

Most parents we spoke to said they felt in some way responsible when they learned their child had a learning disability.

"If I had been a better parent, would he still have these problems?"

"Did I do something wrong?"

Maybe they had learning disabilities themselves and believed their child inherited their weaknesses. "Did he get it from me?" they ask themselves.

Maybe the mothers didn't always follow their doctor's orders during pregnancy. Maybe they smoked, or maybe they took aspirins for headaches. Maybe they had wine with dinner. After the child was born, maybe the mother worked outside the home. Maybe the parents couldn't always be at home after school. Maybe they didn't read to their child enough. Maybe they didn't love the child enough. Maybe, maybe, maybe... Parents told us the "maybes" drove them nuts. There were just too many of them.

Most parents also grieve. Though they haven't physically lost their child, they thought they would have to say goodbye to many of the plans they had for their child.

"Why me? Why is this happening to my child?"

"Why can't he be more like other children?"

"Now she will never go to college. How can I explain this to my parents?"

Parents told us they thought they would have to let go of all of the positive expectations they had for their child. They told us they believed their child would never be "normal" or have a "normal" life. Sometimes they lost hope.

Surprisingly, many parents said they felt relieved.

"I had known for years that there was something wrong with my son. No one would listen to me. I felt my instincts were validated when my son's learning disabilities were diagnosed. I knew a proper evaluation was necessary before he would receive the help he needed."

Many parents said they had worried for a long time, and often their suspicions were much worse than anything the tests revealed. They thought their child was retarded, or they thought their child was lazy, or they thought their child was obnoxious, sometimes even cruel.

Another typical reaction is a feeling of powerlessness, an out-of-control feeling. Parents said they felt paralyzed. "Tell me what to do. I'm not sure where to begin," was a frequent response.

"Do I have to make a decision today?"

"You are the professionals. I'll do whatever you say."

These responses are typical.

Some parents said they believed they were required to do whatever an evaluator recommended if they wanted their child to receive special services. Others thought their child would be removed from the school system if they did not agree with the system's recommended educational plan. Some said they worried that the school staff would insist that their child repeat his current grade and that they would be powerless to refuse.

Many parents said they felt overwhelmed.

"I walked into a room full of specialists. I felt like I had gone to a foreign country. They weren't speaking any language I recognized. Then they handed me a twenty-page report to read and I didn't know what half the words meant. I left that meeting feeling so inadequate."

Just walking into a room filled with special educators can feel pretty intimidating. Many said they felt uncomfortable knowing a roomful of strangers had examined their child and their family. They felt as if their privacy had been violated. Many parents said they were afraid of what they would hear.

There they are, all in one small room. The teacher has an opinion, the counselor has an opinion, the psychologist has something to say, the reading specialist has something to add. Then the special needs teacher presents her findings, and the parent is presented with a multipage document describing the child's special needs. Parents said they felt outnumbered and ill prepared to respond.

The parents we spoke to said they had traveled the emotional path from denial through anger, from anger to guilt, from guilt to powerlessness, from powerlessness through inadequacy. Some emotions became less intense as parents learned more about their child's specific learning disability. But just as often other emotions surfaced or resurfaced.

These emotions are normal. Don't judge yourself too harshly if you are going through this emotional roller coaster. Instead, recognize your child's strengths and accept his limitations. Take time to grieve. Discovering your child has a learning disability can be a sad time. Goals may have to be redefined and compromises may be necessary. Maybe the child you hoped would grow up to be a doctor will grow up to be an artist instead. Maybe instead of an accountant, your child will grow up to be a librarian. Maybe your child won't go to Harvard. Is it really that important? Give yourself time to get used to the idea, but move on.

Anger is a normal emotion. In many ways frustrations go with the territory. Parent support groups can provide tremendous relief and validation when you are feeling angry. Many parents channel their anger into productive areas. One parent we spoke to was motivated to return to school and get her teaching certificate. Another increased her knowledge of learning disabilities sufficiently to become an advocate for other parents.

The learning disability is not your fault. It's not anyone's fault. This fact is particularly hard to accept. Most parents said at some point they felt they were at least indirectly responsible for their children's learning disabilities. Those who had experienced learning problems themselves suspected they passed the genes along to their children. Most came to realize that even if they did, they didn't do it on purpose. And those with learning disabilities in their personal history came to realize they could identify with their child's problems better than most parents. Those who have been there become some of the strongest advocates.

Single parents told us that guilt and blame become larger issues in families when the parents are separated or divorced. One parent often blames the other, and this can create anxious feelings for everyone. Extended families can help most by trying to put differences aside in order to help the child; parents who are able to overcome their differences and unite in the support of their child become part of the solution rather than a contributor to the problem.

Denial is one of the most difficult responses to overcome. A learning disability is difficult to accept, but in order for your child to make progress, you need to listen to your child's specialists and listen to your heart. Most mothers we talked to seemed in tune with that inner voice that told them their child needed something more. Once they got beyond the blame and the guilt, they looked at the issue realistically and helped decide what to do about it. Fathers who accept their child's learning disability and join their wives in helping the child create a formidable advocacy team. If you're a dad reading this book, take note. Join the team.

The bottom line is we all want our children to be "perfect," though we might have a difficult time defining just what perfect is.

Most parents know what it's not. Many still believe a child with a learning disability is not "normal."

In fact, children with learning disabilities are as normal as any other children. All children have strengths and weaknesses. All children excel in one area more than another. In a rational way, most parents understand and accept that.

What makes them reluctant to accept the diagnosis is their fear that their son or daughter will be stuck with a label and placed in a classroom that identifies the child as someone who is not "perfect."

As a professional with more than 20 years of experience in the field of special education, I can assure you today's programs for children with learning disabilities are very different from those offered 25 years ago. In the early elementary grades, most children love the extra attention and the special help. They even like being tested. The evaluator constantly tells them what a great job they are doing, and they often get stickers or other rewards for their work.

Children today are not isolated from their peers. Children with mild disabilities are mainstreamed into typical classrooms all day long. Those with moderate to severe problems may be outside of the classroom for portions of the day, but most schools are making every effort to keep them with their classmates as much as possible.

In most communities, educational labels such as "learning disabled" are essential. It is the label that entitles your child to special services and dictates the type of services your child will receive. Labels allow school systems to identify specific problems without identifying specific children. With an identification label, your child will not lose ground in school if you move from town to town or state to state. Special educators recognize and respond to this jargon. It is hard to separate a label from a stigma, but they are not the same. Try to remember, the label is there to help your child.

Older children have the most difficulty with "labeling." Children of middle school age especially want to be as much like their friends as possible. Anything that isolates or separates them is met with resistance.

Your job is to help them understand the importance of the extra help they will receive. They need to understand that as their academic skills are enhanced, their school performance will improve. As their performance improves, their social skills generally improve as well. What you may initially think of as harmful to your child's self-esteem may indeed work in the opposite way.

When working within the special education system, you will find there are always tradeoffs. Your child might miss a social studies lesson to get extra help in reading, for example. What you need to remember is that your child will get much more out of those social studies lessons once his reading skills are strengthened.

Many parents worry that their child's teachers or peers will treat the child differently if he is identified as having a learning disability. Don't they already? Identification of the problem won't make matters worse. It can only make them better. Many students, especially those with attention deficits, have problems in classroom and social situations. The problems probably came long before the diagnosis, and they may continue following the diagnosis. However, once identified, people realize the child is not an obnoxious brat but a child with a problem. Those working with your child will be less likely to discipline and more likely to help.

Teachers are willing to learn more about specific learning disabilities and to modify their classroom programs when they know children are having difficulty. Teachers and specialists will help your child develop the social skills needed to get along better with peers.

In years past, children with learning disabilities were often "held back." Over and over again, teachers tried to teach them things they couldn't learn. The teachers didn't modify their methods, and so nothing changed, but the school systems still expected the children to learn. Not so today. Children with learning disabilities are seldom held back. Specialists know that repeating the same grade won't make the learning disability go away. Teachers are challenged to modify their programs so all students can learn. With the support of special educators, the curriculum is adapted in a way that helps most children succeed. With help, most children progress along with their classmates.

For those children with severe learning disabilities, many schools offer life skills programs in which students learn the everyday skills necessary to become independent.

One of the most difficult adjustments for parents comes in the modification of their goals for their child. It is not unusual for parents to feel disappointed. Imagine going to your favorite restaurant and ordering veal scallopini. When the waiter puts the plate in front of you, you discover rack of lamb. They're both delicious dishes, but you were prepared for the veal.

Many parents need to make a mental shift in their thinking. You might not have been prepared for the lamb, but you find it's wonderful. So it is when you raise children with special needs. You probably came to parenthood with a map in your head for your child's future. Maybe the route will have to be changed, but your child can still reach the destination.

Knowledge is power. Feelings of powerlessness are lessened when parents learn all they can about their child's specific learning disability. The more you learn about your child's disability, the more control you will have over the process. Read all you can on the subject. Talk to other parents who have been through this. Attend your local support groups.

For many children, it is the program, not the goals, that needs to be adjusted. Children with learning disabilities graduate from high school and go to college every year. (See Chapter 14, Finding the Right College). But for some, a change in expectations is necessary. Learning disabled children, even those with severe disabilities, can lead happy and productive lives. Parents need to redefine success. What is a measure of success for one child might not apply to another. How often have we said, "We only want our child to be happy"?

Parents of children with learning disabilities have the same hopes and dreams for their children as other parents. They want them to lead fulfilling and satisfying lives. They want them to be respected by their peers. They want them to be happy and to have friends.

Caring teachers and loving parents can help pave the way, so hop on the steam roller and help smooth the road.

Chapter 3

Self-Esteem

"Too bad for you that you have two smart children and one stupid one," a learning disabled second grader told his mother. Though his intelligence was assessed in the superior range, he didn't feel smart. Another child was sure she went for special help in understanding her social studies because she wasn't as smart as the other students in her class. This sort of thinking is common among students with learning disabilities, and a low sense of self-esteem is the end result.

Children with low self-esteem can exhibit a variety of symptoms. Some, like the young people we mentioned, will tell you when they feel inadequate. Others exhibit their low sense of self-worth in other ways. Some may blame themselves no matter what goes wrong. Others never accept responsibility for their mistakes and prefer to blame others for their problems. We usually notice the class clown who tries to cover his perceived inadequacies with antics, but sometimes we miss the child who always tries to do the right thing. Low self-esteem is often the cause of behavioral problems, not just in school, but in extracurricular activities as well.

Your child may be the one who just can't make friends. He may be the object of cruel teasing, but he may just as likely be the bully who makes life miserable for other children. She may be the one to throw temper tantrums, or in some extreme cases, the one throwing the chair. He may talk nonstop, or he may be reluctant to share his thoughts and ideas.

When discussing self-esteem, it is important to remember that children with learning disabilities are as diverse as children without learning problems. Some enjoy acting, others like baseball. Some excel in art, others like to climb mountains. Some are risk-takers, and some like to stay at home. Their learning disability is only a small part of their makeup.

Unfortunately, since school is such a central part of every child's day, the learning disability often becomes the focus. Students begin to see themselves in this narrowed view as well. They believe that if they are not successful in school, they cannot be successful in social situations either.

Various activities can help boost your child's self-esteem, but as one parent explained, "Until children can see some academic performance—some success—until they start learning to read and feel that gap close, they will not feel good about themselves. Kids know who can and who can't."

This is why your child's educational plan is so important. Start there. Work with your child's team to help your child feel successful in school. That's not always easy. Sometimes it is important to help children with learning disabilities keep the goal in mind. And that goal need not be getting an "A" on a report card. The goal is for your child to learn to compensate for his disabilities.

Though most schools are making every effort to "mainstream" children in the classroom, it is not always in the learning disabled child's best interest. Yes, taking a child out of her regular classroom can make her feel "different," but sometimes having her stay in the classroom confirms those differences. You don't want your child forced into situations where she cannot possibly measure up. Sometimes, especially in the lower grades, students are more likely to take educational risks, to challenge themselves, to try new things when they don't have to worry about how their classmates will react.

Though children sometimes resist this type of educational model, it can be effective.

One specialist we spoke to presents it to her students this way when they are reluctant to go for special help: "If you had a broken leg, you would go to see the doctor. If your ears were growing backwards, you would go to a specialist and have them turned around. You would do what you could to make yourself more alike than different."

She tells them working on skills development should be viewed in the same way. When your child receives extra services in school, you can help him see it as part of the road to success. As one parent put it, "The road might be bumpy, but you learn to ride bumpy roads."

Since so much focus is placed on academic achievement in school, try to place your emphasis on the child's efforts toward the goal instead of on the achievement of the goal.

Unless it is part of the educational plan, try to separate home life from school life. While your child is working to succeed in school, make home a place where he feels secure and accepted. Students with learning disabilities have weaknesses in their academics, but they usually have strengths in other areas that can help them feel successful. Help your child find those areas. Some, as we mentioned, excel at sports. Just as often, however, the group activities often associated with childhood are not good places for children with learning disabilities. Though your child may be well coordinated and athletic, complex team sports can present opportunities for failure. When directions are shouted, some children have trouble absorbing the message, breaking it down, and carrying it out quickly enough to respond in time. Choreographed movements on a football field may have no meaning to children with spatial problems.

Most of the parents we spoke to said their children excelled when they were involved in individual athletic activities or in activities that had individual components. Horseback riding, karate, swimming, fencing, bowling, dancing, gymnastics, hiking, and skiing are sports where athletic children with learning disabilities can excel.

Those who do not enjoy sports can find an outlet for their talents in the arts. Drawing, painting, sculpting, photography, acting, singing, and dancing are excellent choices.

We need to adjust our thinking and question our values. Most of us look at these alternative activities as somehow less important than the academic work that goes on in school. Somehow we think being successful in the arts or in sports has less value than being successful in school. These achievements should be valued as highly as any academic success. If we don't do that, we give our children less than they deserve.

When children feel less than adequate, they often have trouble in social situations. They don't make friends easily. They don't work well in groups. They don't know how to approach others, and they don't know how to respond. They are sometimes ridiculed and sometimes isolated.

These are the incidents that move parents to tears for their children. Unfortunately, parents can't "buy" friends for their children. In fact, that approach often backfires. The mother who invites the entire class to the pool for an afternoon also invites disaster. Children are savvy social animals. They know when children can't make friends on their own. A large group gathered poolside will provide them with another chance to interact with each other without including your child. No matter how subtle you feel you are, your child sees your involvement as confirmation of her belief that she cannot handle social situations on her own.

Instead, help your child explore options for group activities. Boy Scouts, Girl Scouts, church clubs, YMCAs, and museum workshops provide a variety of group-related activities. You set up the opportunities, but your child makes the choice. Give him the opportunity to make the decision and you have made him feel more independent and responsible for a successful outcome.

Acknowledge to yourself and to your child that things won't always go well. They don't always go well for children without learning disabilities, and they don't always go well for children who have learning problems. You can't take all the hurt away. Talk openly about the disability and the way it affects the child's life.

One parent explained, "My son had to face being so smart, yet defeated. He wondered why it came so much easier to everyone else. Now we have come past blame and punishment, and I can talk to him. Now he understands. He doesn't like it, but he understands."

One of the additional difficulties faced by those with learning disabilities is that they are in some ways programmed to expect failure. Their way of looking at things can sometimes take on a level of suspicion and distrust. An unkind remark will bounce off a child with a strong sense of self-esteem, but that same remark is viewed as a personal and destructive attack by a child who is already feeling vulnerable.

When a child accidentally moved a chair and caused another student to fall recently, everyone in the classroom recognized the incident as an accident—everyone except the learning disabled child who fell to the floor. She was convinced the other child did it intentionally because he wanted to hurt her, because he didn't like her, because he thought she deserved it, because she was not as good as the other children, because she was dumb.

It is important not to trivialize children's feelings, however. Sometimes the emotional involvement and lack of self-esteem grow to such a level that children and families need professional help. Children with low self-esteem may be vulnerable to psychological problems including depression, sleep disorders, eating disorders, and drug and alcohol problems.

Sometimes parents minimize these feelings of hopelessness, helplessness, frustration, and anxiety. They view the difficulties as short-term and think they will go away when the situation causing them is addressed. That's not always true. If your child makes self-injurious statements, his physical appearance changes, his school performance drops precipitously, his friends change, or he becomes isolated, you should consult a mental health specialist. Your school guidance counselor or your family physician can help you find someone to provide support for your child and your family.

Elevating a child's self-esteem is a long-term process. Don't expect to make changes or see improvements overnight. Just as a learning disability is a continuous educational challenge, issues of self-esteem will continue to be a source of concern. Anything you can do to help your child feel secure, loved, and valued will be worth the effort. A strong sense of self-esteem will contribute to every facet of your child's life.

Chapter 4

Home Life

Malcolm's mother called him inside for the fifth time. He was playing stickball with his friends and really didn't want to leave the game. It was a beautiful day, and he seemed to be having so much fun. She hated to make him come in and sit at the kitchen table. Unfortunately, his teacher had sent a note home that afternoon saying his mother should supervise his homework. She knew Malcolm needed help with his lessons, but why did she have to be the one to help? Whenever she tried to help him, they ended up shouting at each other. The last time they worked together, both ended up in tears. If Malcolm was having trouble with his math lessons, why didn't his teacher do something about it? That was her job. Shouldn't Malcolm have learned how to do these problems in school? Wasn't homework supposed to be simply practice? She had enough to do working all day, shopping, keeping the house clean, fixing meals, and caring for her children. Why did she have to be a tutor, too?

Malcolm's teacher didn't see things in quite the same way. She had 30 children in her classroom. Several, like Malcolm, needed special attention. If she spent all her time teaching them, the other 26 children would fall behind. Parents are supposed to support their children, the teacher believed, and Malcolm's mother could easily help him with his homework. That was her job. Unfortunately,

Malcolm's teacher didn't realize the kind of stress she was placing on Malcolm's family by insisting his mother help with his schoolwork.

Homework is just one of many stressful issues faced by the families of learning disabled children. Coping with the many issues that must be addressed often creates disharmony in the happiest of homes. One of the most common causes of stress in the household is fatigue.

Parents of children with learning disabilities are tired. In addition to the normal stresses of family life, they are continually working on their child's behalf. They mediate, advocate, intervene, referee, plan, negotiate, and adapt until they are exhausted. In the meantime, they provide emotional support for their learning disabled child, while trying to balance the attention given that child with the attention given the other members of the family. No wonder they are worn out.

"There are times when I lose it. I have been known to call him a jerk to his face," one mother told us.

She was not an exception. Most parents "lose it" once in while. Don't be too hard on yourself if it happens to you. You won't always make the right decisions. No one does. Be willing to say, "I made a mistake."

Try to find some time for yourself. It's difficult with all there is to do, but even a few minutes of personal time can help alleviate some of the stress.

One parent we spoke to said she could not function without a stress-relieving morning walk. She meets with friends each day before her children are out of bed and gets a good start to the day. Any type of physical exercise can help. Another parent spends those early-morning moments reading a favorite author. Getting up a little early is not painful when you are spending that time doing something you really enjoy.

If yours is a two-parent household, try to divide some of the more stressful activities. Sometimes one parent is more ready and able to cope than another. Make adjustments and share the responsibilities.

If you can afford one, having a baby-sitter assume responsibility for your children one or two afternoons a week can provide much-needed relief. Some parents we spoke to had the sitter care for one child while they used the time for a little one-on-one activity with another child. If you can't afford to pay for child care, perhaps you can switch off with a friend or neighbor.

Go to bed early. Most of the parents we spoke to said that was an essential ingredient in having the energy to make it through the day.

Join a support group. Parents told us they found enormous validation and comfort among other parents who understood the stresses of working with learning disabled children. In some states, school systems are required to help form these parent support groups. If your system doesn't have one, start one. It will be worth the effort.

Every family's level of tolerance for conflict is different. If you are in a situation where the degree of conflict is escalating, it is time to talk to someone. If you catch the situation early enough, the intervention does not have to be long term—brief therapy or therapy during certain stages of development can be very helpful. If you begin to feel out of control, seek professional help.

"Get help the minute you come to terms with the fact that you need support," one parent advised. "When the milk flows out of the glass, you have filled it too much and you need help," she said.

If you are worried about paying for that type of help, check with your community mental health agencies. Most have sliding fee scales based on income. Many insurance companies cover this type of service. When your life is out of control, you cannot consider this type of service a luxury. It is essential.

Activities that cause normal stress in most homes cause an extraordinary level of stress in homes of children with learning disabilities. Homework is a stressful issue in most families, but when your child is learning disabled, the simplest assignment can become a nightmare. Most children with learning disabilities work extra hard in school just to keep up with their classmates. Then, when they get home, teachers expect them to sit down with their parents to work some more. They are already tired, and their parents are tired, too. This is when parents need to make accommodations and adaptations to help things progress more smoothly.

Organization and structure help most children with learning disabilities. Most households are centers of chaos. Children's activities are juggled with mealtimes, and schedules are shifted as different needs arise. Most families with learning disabled children find they cannot survive in that type of environment. While it is difficult at first, you must make your home life more structured. While schedules may seem rigid, the benefits will soon become obvious.

Parents of children with learning disabilities told us structure is essential. Set aside a specific time and place for homework assignments, and let your child know you are going to stick to the plan. Sometimes your child's best time for doing assignments is not your best time to work with her. Whenever possible, work during your child's best time. If she is less frustrated, it is likely you will be less frustrated as well.

Tools can be especially helpful for children with a learning disability. A typewriter or word processor can end the constant frustration of a child who has trouble with penmanship. A word processor with a spell checker can make life a lot more pleasant for a child with spelling disabilities. A calculator can be a source of joy to a child with math problems.

Organization can also help. Assign your child a place to keep all school-related materials—books, homework, school notices, lunch money, supplies. Mornings will run more smoothly if all school things are kept in one place.

Family Relationships— Mothers Get Involved

When a child has a learning disability, the entire family is affected. Mothers are often the most involved in the day-to-day issues. They are usually the ones who meet with the teachers, drive to the doctors, and consult with the specialists. Most often it is the mother who listens when the child is hurt, who intervenes when there are social problems, and who acts as referee among the other family members. Moms are often exhausted. That is not to say that fathers are totally removed from the picture. Some dads pitch in. Unfortunately, in most families we spoke to, fathers took on a secondary role.

Fathers Need Convincing

Sometimes fathers themselves present a problem. Fathers, as we discussed in Chapter 2, often have difficulty accepting that their child has a learning disability. They want their child to be perfect, and they have trouble accepting any kind of compromise that addresses the child's particular learning style or learning needs.

Because many fathers of learning disabled youngsters had learning disabilities themselves, they often respond by saying, "I made it through and I didn't need any help. If my kid weren't so lazy he would make it through." This type of response is part of the denial.

Sometimes it is difficult for fathers to acknowledge their child has a problem because the child has two behavior patterns—one for when his mother is around, and another for when his father is there. Lots of times children are really horrendous to those who are with them all day. In most families, the dads tend to see the children for much shorter periods of time.

In any case, it is hard for families to work together if the father won't acknowledge the child's problem.

"The first step is convincing your husband that your child has a learning disability. You must convince him before anyone else. Now my husband is a real advocate," one mother said.

As that mother noted, when fathers become directly involved in the process, they often come around. When they are involved as part of the educational team, they understand the issues involved in educating a child with special needs, and they become more supportive. Sometimes their involvement helps them overcome their guilt, grief, and/or denial. Often they want to take a more active role in their child's growth and development.

"In some families the duties are shared, but most of the time it is moms who get involved. Parents who truly share the responsibility on a fifty-fifty basis are still in the minority. Our goal is to mobilize the entire family and to draw on everyone's strengths," a school psychologist said.

Involving Fathers

How can mothers involve fathers in the process?

Try to schedule team meetings at times when both parents can attend. It is often possible to hold meetings early in the morning or late in the afternoon. When both parents attend meetings, there are four ears instead of two absorbing all the information the team has to offer. Make sure fathers are involved whenever the child sees a specialist. When he can't be there, be sure he has a chance to see copies of all reports. When families face these issues together, parents can offer each other comfort and support. Everyone ends up feeling better about the possibilities for success.

Ask other members of your support group how they share responsibilities in their families. Don't be afraid to admit that your husband is reluctant to become involved. Most families have addressed this issue at some time during their child's education.

Fathers should be encouraged to attend parent support group meetings.

"Maybe I would go if there were other fathers there," one dad said.

Support group organizers would do well to address the needs of the fathers by holding special fathers' evenings or inviting speakers to address issues of particular interest to dads. Make that suggestion at your support group meetings.

One of the saddest things those of us involved in helping children with learning disabilities observe is the wedge that sometimes comes between parents. The stresses involved in raising a child with learning disabilities can drive parents apart. Family counselors are trained to help deal with these issues. Don't hesitate to seek their help.

Sibling Survival

"Why do you spend so much time helping Jeff with his homework? You never help me! Why is he always such a brat? He breaks my toys. He hides my books. He's a pain! He's a retard and he's driving me crazy!"

Sibling conflict is hard on everyone. Parent energy often is focused on the neediest child. Sometimes brothers and sisters just don't understand why parents have to spend so much time with one child. Often they are jealous.

Occasionally they are embarrassed. Sometimes they must explain to friends why their brother or sister has such a hard time learning. Sometimes they are frightened it could happen to them.

Most of these emotions find their way out—usually in negative ways. The name calling, fighting, and tattling, common in most homes, get magnified in the homes of learning disabled children. There are only 24 hours in a day, and many times the learning disabled child consumes most of them.

Sometimes brothers and sisters who do not have learning disabilities find they have to spend much of their time helping a sibling with a learning disability. Occasionally a child can lose his own childhood caring for another.

Parents can help alleviate some of these difficulties by carefully explaining the situation to all the children. You are not being disloyal by telling the children their brother or sister has learning problems. It helps them understand what is happening in your home.

Though it is difficult, try to schedule some special one-to-one time with the nondisabled child on a regular basis—perhaps one afternoon a week. The anticipation of having that time set aside diminishes some of the anger and jealousy.

Life can be hard for siblings of a learning disabled child, but it is even harder for the child with the learning disability. Imagine struggling all day to write a report. Then a younger brother or sister comes home and whips off an essay on Christopher Columbus without even opening the dictionary. It can be very frustrating.

Report card days are especially unpleasant for learning disabled children. Comparisons are not unusual, and the child with a learning disability does not usually come out on top. It's easy to understand the resentment many of these children feel toward their brothers and sisters.

Just as you reserved a special time to spend with your other children, do something special with your learning disabled child —something she feels successful about.

Don't drive yourself crazy trying to do everything for everyone. It's just not possible. When children complain you are not being fair, try to remember the true meaning of the word. Fair is when everyone gets what he or she needs, not necessarily what he or she wants. Learning disabled children have greater needs. It's really that simple.

The best you can do is to encourage your children to be open and honest about how they feel. When those feelings are suppressed, they often escape in anger. If your learning disabled child sees a counselor or therapist, be sure to include your other children in some of those meetings.

Guiding Grandparents

Brothers and sisters aren't the only ones to react in a family with a learning disabled child. Though grandparents can be most supportive of young children, they frequently do not understand the problems involved in learning disabilities. They do not always have enough information to be of help. Sometimes they actually make matters worse.

Grandparents often believe grandchildren should be raised the way *their* children were raised. If it worked for their children (and obviously it did, they report, because you turned out so great), then it should work for your children too. They don't understand learning disabilities, especially the behavior problems often associated with attention deficit disorder (ADD), and they can be very critical.

"Send them to me for a week or two. I'll straighten them out," is a simplification often heard from grandparents.

One parent we spoke to had a terrific solution to this dilemma. She told us she gathered material about her child's learning disability and gave it to her parents. "Unless you are willing to read this material, please don't say anything," she told them.

For her family, it worked. The grandparents became interested in learning disabilities and became advocates for their grandchild.

Some families have found it helpful to include a grandparent in team meetings. This is especially helpful if grandparents are frequently caregivers or baby-sitters. Team meetings will help them understand the complexity of a learning disability and help them understand some of the issues you face each day.

Social Struggles

If relationships within the family are hard for children with learning disabilities, those outside the home can present even greater problems. Children with poor verbal skills and little understanding of body language have a hard time making friends. Children with ADD are often impulsive and need to learn to monitor their fists and their mouths. When children are frustrated all day long in their learning environment, it is hard for them to get along socially at the end of the day.

These social struggles present a problem not only for your child, but for you as well. Most parents of children with learning disabilities have watched in agony as their child was ridiculed by others. It's painful for the child, and it's painful for the parent.

Unfortunately, there are no easy solutions to these complex problems. You can try to involve your child in activities that develop self-esteem. Your local mental health agency or your school's guidance office can be a good source of information on this type of activity. As your child's self-esteem improves, her relationships will as well (see Chapter 3).

Small group activities work best for most LD children. Instead of inviting several children over to play in hopes your child will "hit it off" with one of them, invite one child. If it goes well, great. If it doesn't, try a different child.

As much as possible, help your child learn to roll with the punches, but make sure your child can come to you when social situations become intolerable. If he has difficulty expressing his hurt, have him put his feelings down on paper with words or drawings. Take the time to talk about how he feels.

Dealing with Discipline

Just as your child has exceptional learning needs, you will find you have exceptional obligations when it comes to disciplining.

"Whatever problems you have with regular kids, you have them worse with learning disabled children. Parents of children with learning disabilities have a greater responsibility to persevere and not give up," one parent said.

Most parents we spoke to were quick to agree. One piece of advice that came from many parents of learning disabled children was summed up by the parent of an ADD child: "Do not let them off the hook because they have a learning disability," she said.

Learning disabled children need structure, structure, structure. They need to know not only what the rules are, but how to follow them as well. Don't merely tell them what not to do. Tell them and show them how you want them to behave. Once you have established your expectations, discipline must be highly organized. You have to hold your ground.

"Be real clear you are the parent—make no excuses or apologies for that. Let them know what you value and what you do not. I don't care what people next door do or think. This is not my concern," one parent said.

Flexibility and compromise are not sensible approaches when dealing with learning disabled children, parents said.

Many in their frustration vacillate between making unreasonable allowances for their children's disability and expecting them to behave as if they had no problems at all. Or, they allow themselves to be manipulated by the child, and then get angry and punitive. It is not always easy to be consistent. But that works best.

"If you start arguing, you are lost," another parent said.

Spend some time focusing on what goes well. So often we get consumed by all the things that need to be corrected, we forget to stop and congratulate ourselves or our children when we do something especially well. If you make an effort to catch your child doing something well, you may not need to do so much disciplining.

Many children with learning disabilities need extra time to follow directions. They sometimes get angry when they are expected to respond immediately. Don't expect them to jump the moment you ask them to clean up or get ready.

Children with learning disabilities are usually not very good at planning ahead. You can help them by giving them ample warning when you want them to do something.

"I give him a little extra warning." one parent advised. "I say, 'In five minutes we have to clean up.' "

Keeping Records

Just as children need to keep themselves and their work organized, parents must find a way to keep information related to their child's disability in an appropriate place. The Massachusetts Federation for Children with Special Needs recommends keeping a home file. They suggest materials be kept in chronological order. Each year's list should include the names of your child's teacher, school, principal, psychologist, special education teacher(s), school district superintendent, school board members, and the special education administrator. Include phone numbers where appropriate.

Keep a copy of the state and local regulations in the file as well. The file should include copies of all your child's school records, including report cards. Copies of test results as well as recommendations from independent assessments should be kept together in the file. A complete list of your child's medications and a copy of his educational plan should also be kept in the file.

Organization helps everyone involved with the special education process. Children with learning disabilities function best when their lives are structured and their parents' responses are predictable. Family members respond most positively when they understand the effects of learning disabilities and can anticipate the learning disabled child's reactions and behaviors. A structured, cooperative environment can make home a safe, nurturing, and noncompetitive place for a learning disabled child, and that environment can have a positive effect on the entire family.

Chapter 5

Adolescence

Phoebe took the letters from the mailbox. Her heart sank when she saw the return address of the high school. They never sent good news.

Her son Adam was a freshman. He liked doing his work independently and resented it when she asked to see his assignments. According to Adam, he was doing fine in school.

Unfortunately, that's not what the letter said. Adam's special education teacher reported he was not making progress. His homework assignments were not complete. He was not going to many of his classes, and when he did show up for class, his teachers reported his attitude was bad.

Many children with learning disabilities find the transition to the upper grades extremely difficult. Even those who learned to compensate well for their disabilities in the elementary and middle school grades often find the increased workload and teaching style in high school overwhelming. High school students, and to a certain extent middle school students, want to be like everyone else. They don't want special help. They don't want modifications in their program of studies. In fact, they don't want to stand out in any way. Because they find it difficult to accept help, they often find themselves falling behind and sometimes even failing.

The social pressures on middle and high school students are enormous. They are worried about their clothes. They are worried about their skin. They are thinking more about their hair than their homework. They are dealing with other issues—just like all the other students in the upper grades. What is unfortunate is that middle and high school students with special needs don't always have the time to focus their attention on these adolescent problems. They have to give more of their attention to their academics than do those students who do not have difficulty learning. Many adolescents can spend three hours on the telephone and one hour on their homework and get by. Most students with special needs can't.

Academic problems often begin to grow during the middle school years and accelerate as the students enter high school. In the early grades, students usually have the same teacher all day for all subjects. If reading group is held in the morning and your child doesn't finish all of her work, she might have time later in the day to complete it.

Things are different at the high school level. Students are expected to do more in less time. High school classes are broken up by content, and a student must finish all class work within the allotted class time or else bring it home.

If students need special help in the elementary grades, it can be worked into their schedules. In many communities support services are provided within the regular classroom. This doesn't happen in most middle schools or high schools. If a student needs extra help, he is expected to seek it out. No one will be looking for him during lunch or after school to be sure he completes his assignment. Students are expected to work independently.

During the elementary years, children are learning to learn. Teachers strive to teach the learning process, to develop solid study skills necessary for learning. By the time students are in high school, the teachers expect them to have acquired these skills and be ready to apply them to the content areas.

Elementary school teachers are specialists in accommodating a variety of learning styles. Elementary teachers lecture, they write on the board, they provide students with hands-on activities, they use books with pictures, they read aloud and encourage students to read aloud, they sing. Children can absorb information through their eyes, their ears, their hands.

Things are different at the high school. Most teachers expect students to adapt to their teaching style, not the other way around. They have a content to teach and only 40 minutes to present it. They may teach as many as 150 students each day, and they aren't given the support they need to adapt their lessons to a variety of learning styles. It's difficult for the teacher.

It's even more difficult for the child with a learning disability. Many high school classes are lecture based. The teacher talks and the student listens. He writes down what the teachers say, and gives it back to them on the quarterly test or in a written project. But what about the student who has difficulty writing, or the student who learns best with visual clues, or the student who has trouble reading 30 pages of literature a night?

A typical student with four or five major subjects must adjust to four or five different teaching styles. Each of the teachers will have specific expectations. One wants the homework done in a spiral notebook—"only write on one side of the page, please." Another wants her assignments completed in ink—blue or black, period. Still another says to do calculations in pencil and use graph paper when necessary. It's a wonder anyone can keep it all straight. Now add an organizational disability to the picture, and you can imagine the nightmare. If you are the parent of a high school student, you probably won't need your imagination.

By the time a student graduates from high school, she is expected to have a fund of information about the world. She is also expected to be able to apply inferential reasoning skills in order to sequence, understand abstract concepts, distinguish important from unimportant details, and understand cause and effect. She is expected to be able to remember what she has learned and to organize information in meaningful units. She is also expected to be able to attend to tasks for at least a full class period.

For the eleventh grade student who is still reading on a fifth or sixth grade level, this all seems like an impossible task. It is no wonder that the first thing to go, if it was intact before, is the student's self-esteem.

Unfortunately, a drop in feelings of self-worth is often accompanied by absenteeism and a change in behavior. For many students, the place that once provided the three R's now seems to focus on the three D's: discipline, demerits, and detention.

This shift in focus is even anticipated in the federal regulations governing special education. The special education law acknowledges that a child with a learning disability cannot be educated properly if he is not in school. If that child is suspended for behavioral problems, he is not only being suspended from his regular classes, he is being denied his special education services as well. Federal regulations won't allow that to happen without a great deal of meeting time and red tape.

So what are parents to do? Teachers and experienced parents tell us that what parents can't do is give up.

One of the best things parents can do comes directly from the scouting manual—Be Prepared! You've heard all the horror stories. Don't assume there is nothing you can do.

When your child enters high school, talk to his teachers. Most high school teachers we talked to said they seldom hear from the parents of their students. By the time most students get to the high school, their parents have attended 8 holiday concerts, 32 parent conferences, 150 sporting events, numerous bake sales and PTA meetings, and at least 8 open houses. They have chaperoned dozens of field trips, volunteered an average of 288 hours, baked 192 cookies. In their spare time they led scout troops, coached baseball teams, acted as chauffeurs, made costumes for pageants, all while working full time. It's really not surprising that they begin to be less involved.

As the parents of a student with learning disabilities, however, this is not your time to relax. Sorry.

Make sure you know your school's special needs coordinator. It helps to have someone who knows your child well acting in his behalf.

When your child enters high school, contact each of her teachers. Let them know where your child's strengths and weaknesses fall. You will give them a head start in getting to know your child and help them anticipate difficulties that might arise.

"If you know your son has trouble sitting through a forty-minute class without moving around, tell me at the start of the year," one teacher said. "Don't wait until I call you to say your son just can't sit still in class. You already know that."

Make sure your child gets to school. Teachers tell us that there are many strategies for helping a high school student with learning disabilities succeed in classes, but they need the student in school to accomplish this. They realize that it is very difficult to force a teenager to attend school, but they are willing to work with parents to try to help. The most important thing, they say, is to make sure the student doesn't give up. Once students give up on school, it is very difficult to get them back.

If truancy is a major issue for your child, explore alternative programs. Many schools offer work/study arrangements; small, structured programs; and/or other programs specifically designed to prevent dropouts.

Don't skip that open house or teacher's meeting. It really helps for the teachers to have a face to put with a parent's name—to have a personality to relate to. It sends a message to your child as well. If you are willing to rush through supper after a long day to hear about his progress, he knows you care about his education.

Homework creates problems for most parents of special needs students throughout their academic careers. At the middle school and high school level, homework becomes an incendiary device. Bring up the subject at the next parent support meeting and see how volatile the discussion becomes!

Special education teachers recommend that parents stay involved in the homework process but take on a different role. Older students don't want their parents looking over their shoulders while they do their assignments. They resent the intrusion. It is better for the parent to take a step back and act as facilitator rather than supervisor.

Special education teachers give the following advice: Provide your child with an organized space to do her work. Make sure she has the materials she will need to complete the work. If she is working on geometry, make sure she has a compass. If she is writing an essay for social studies, make sure there is a dictionary nearby. Don't accept "I can't find a pen" as an excuse. Make sure there are plenty of pens and pencils handy.

Though you can't check every homework item your child must complete, you should make it part of your daily routine to check his assignment notebook. Be skeptical when your child says, "I don't have any homework." If he knows you know what is expected, he will be more likely to try to complete his assignments.

Let your child know that effort is important. If she is struggling with a concept or a problem, don't let her get away with using "I don't get it" as an excuse for not doing the assignment. Most teachers respect a student who will make an effort, especially when they know the student is struggling.

Involve your child as much as possible in the process. Don't make promises to teachers for him without consulting him first. Most school systems encourage student involvement in annual special education review meetings. Your child should be part of the team and should help develop his educational plan.

If you know your child is having trouble and that a meeting will involve a negative report, perhaps you could meet with the teachers first to discuss your child's progress. Schedule a second team meeting with your child present and give him a brief review of the first meeting. He will then have an opportunity to present his ideas in a positive environment.

If his behavioral problems are severe, it is possible that his educational plan is not addressing his behavioral/emotional needs adequately. If your child's behavioral problems are related to his learning disability, his educational plan should be amended to address those issues. The educational plan should include strategies for dealing with the student's behavior.

Adolescents don't like having other people know about issues that involve their emotions. They want to hide anything that sets them apart from other teenagers, those they consider "normal" students. Most students don't realize that "normal" people get help every day—it's not just the "losers" or the "screwed-up" people who need counseling.

Many schools have counselors who specialize in working with adolescents with special needs, and most community mental health agencies have people with experience in working with young people.

Some schools offer group counseling sessions during the school day. Many students are very receptive to this approach. If your middle school or high school does not offer this type of counseling, you might want to help get a program organized.

High school students are often so busy living in the moment that they find it difficult to look ahead. This attitude comes in direct conflict with the view of most parents, who tend to look ahead. They want to know what is going to happen once their child graduates from high school.

Most parents don't know that special education services are available until a child is 22 or until he graduates from high school. Your child does not have to finish high school in four years. He doesn't have to graduate at 18. Maybe he will be a more successful student if he takes a reduced course load and spreads it out over five or six years. This possibly should be discussed carefully with the special education staff at your child's school to determine what would be gained by exercising this option.

College is an option for many students with learning disabilities (see Chapter 14). If your child wants to go to college, she should begin to discuss this with her special education teacher as early as possible during her high school years. Many steps must be followed in order to qualify as an applicant with a learning disability. There are also procedures to be followed for taking admissions tests for college. Make sure she doesn't miss out on this opportunity because she missed the deadline for completing the necessary paperwork. The college search itself might take more than a year.

Not every student goes to college. Not every student wants to go to college. Many students with learning disabilities graduate from high school and enter trade schools or go directly into the job market. When thinking ahead, be sure to consider your child's abilities and interests realistically.

Adolescence causes some turmoil in most families. Difficulties can last a few months (if you're lucky) or they can go on for a few years. While these young people are still *your* children, they are no longer children. Those problems that could be treated with a hug when the child was in third grade just can't be handled that way anymore. Many adolescents need a hug, but they won't allow you to be in the same room with them long enough to give them one. Adolescence is hard for them, and it's very hard for their parents. Hold on and do the best you can. Battle-scarred parents report they survived. You will too.

Chapter 6

The Team Approach

Margaret was concerned about her son Derek's progress in school. Suspecting he might have a learning disability, she approached the classroom teacher to discuss it. The teacher agreed, saying Derek was not paying attention in class, and he was having difficulty learning to read and write. They agreed that an evaluation was in order, and Margaret gave the okay for the necessary tests.

Neither Margaret nor the teacher was surprised when the tests indicated Derek had a learning disability that was making it difficult for him to learn to read. The school recommended special help. Margaret agreed, but said she felt there might be another problem as well. She suspected Derek might have an attention deficit disorder (ADD) and said she would like to consult a neurologist. The neurologist confirmed Margaret's suspicions and prescribed the stimulant medication Ritalin to help Derek focus his attention.

By working together, Derek's mother, the classroom teacher, the special education teacher, and the neurologist helped Derek succeed in school.

Margaret's role was not an unusual one. As a parent, she knew more about her child than anyone—more than the teachers, more than the therapists, more than the neurologist. Each of them had important information about Derek, but she was the one who helped pull all that fragmented information together. She helped the team view Derek as a whole child.

As the parent of a child with a learning disability, you too will want to be a part of your child's educational team. In order to do that, you need to do two things. First, you need to learn as much as you can about your child's specific learning disability. The more you know, the more you will be able to understand your child's special needs.

Second, you need to develop a successful working relationship with the professionals in your school system who are helping your child. You want your child's teachers to view you as an essential part of the team.

Strange as it may seem, some professionals view parent involvement as a threat. Help them see you in a positive light, as a source of information and support.

The professionals on your child's team might include a physician, a psychologist, the classroom teacher, the school nurse, the special education teacher, an occupational therapist, a physical therapist, and a speech and language therapist. The combination of professionals on your child's team will be determined by his specific learning disability.

The physician might monitor your child's physical health and may prescribe medications if necessary. If medications are prescribed, the school nurse will be involved in administering them. A psychologist, counselor, or social worker might help monitor your child's emotional development and will help foster his self-esteem. Therapists may act as consultants or may provide direct services to help strengthen your child's specific areas of muscular weakness. Special education teachers may help strengthen your child's academic skills and help him compensate for weaknesses. In most cases, the classroom teacher will be the most involved with your child. For that reason, that is the best place to start if you have questions or problems.

One parent who has fought many special education battles told us, "Teachers are very willing to work with you, but you need to make the effort. I say, 'If there is anything I can do, let me know.' I am not an expert, but I want to share with the teacher what I know about my child."

Communications with teachers and specialists work best when parents take a positive attitude. Let them know you are not there to challenge their judgment, but to help them see things about your child that might not be obvious in a school setting.

You may not always agree with your child's teacher, but you both have your child's best interest at heart. Listen carefully to the teacher and share your insights. It is helpful to try to see both sides of an issue.

Though parents are sometimes reluctant to tell teachers they are having trouble working with their child at home, it is essential. Teachers can't know what is going on at home unless you tell them. They may be sending home work and expecting you to help your child with it. If your helping creates large-scale battles, the teacher needs to know that. Perhaps your responsibility should be to provide the child with a disruption-free environment rather than actually sitting and working with him. With an open relationship, you and the teacher may develop compromises that work best for everyone.

Most parents have mixed feelings when they become involved as part of the team. Some parents are fearful the teacher will blame them for their child's problem. They feel if they are part of the team they must be willing to do their part at home, no matter what is suggested. Some parents feel resentful because they have to become "teachers" as well as parents. They feel they have more than enough to do in helping their child without having to drill her in her math skills as well. How can they be a team player if they are having these feelings?

Parents who work closely with the classroom teacher usually find those feelings unfounded. With their involvement, they help the teacher understand the energy and effort involved in parenting a child with a learning disability. Sometimes one more responsibility is more than the most dedicated parent can handle. Once you have developed a good working relationship with your child's teacher, he or she will understand that.

If you find, despite your best efforts, that you are unable to work with your child's classroom teacher, keep in mind that other specialists are working with your child as well. They are there to help your child, and they are there to help you. A group meeting can be used to develop a plan that will work for you and your child. These meetings can also resolve communication problems among members of the team.

The most difficult issue parents face as part of the team comes when they don't agree with the team's decisions about their child. It is difficult to balance your role as your child's primary advocate with your role as a team player. Parents tell us there are times when they need to become more assertive.

Once your child's learning disability has been identified, your child has specific rights (see Chapter 15), and you have an obligation to see that your child receives the services he needs. Just because you disagree with the other members of your child's team doesn't mean they don't want what's best for your child. They care. They just don't agree with you.

This type of adversarial situation creates additional stress for parents and teachers. Sometimes the stress is released with anger. Parents told us they sometimes fell into the trap of treating the other members of the team as enemies. This approach is seldom successful, they said. Through the determination and patience, it is possible to continue to reach your goals without unreasonable charges, demands, or threats.

Instead of saying, "I'll take you to court if I don't get what I want," try saying, "There are some things in my child's educational plan that I would like to see changed. Can we get together to talk about them?" If your requests are not met in a reasonable amount of time and with understanding, you may have to become more firm. If necessary, you might say, "I understand my rights and I intend to see my child receives the services he deserves."

The first statement lets the professionals know you understand the law and how to make it work for you, but the second statement will probably be better received. The third statement lets them know you are very serious and expect a timely response to your concerns.

Attack issues, not people. Instead of saying, "You're a rotten teacher. If you could teach, my child wouldn't be having these problems," try saying, "I feel Johnny's needs could be better addressed by another approach."

Perhaps you can help the teacher grow in understanding of your child's specific learning disability by sharing information you have found helpful.

Sometimes parents feel they are under attack when working with the teacher. Instead of saying, "Get off my back. This isn't all my fault," try, "I feel I am being blamed for my child's disability. Let's focus on helping my child instead of placing blame."

Some parents we spoke to said their emotional involvement sometimes got in the way of their objectivity when listening to recommendations. Sometimes the information was so complicated they had difficulty following. In these situations, an extra set of ears can be helpful. One parent we spoke to brought along a neighbor who could talk with her after the meeting to help her zero in on issues she herself might have missed. Another parent brought her mother. She knew that she would have to go over everything with her mother after the meeting anyway, so she made the task easier for herself. Sometimes just having an objective person listen to the group discussion and talk about it following the meeting helps clear up misunderstandings or misconceptions.

Other parents have turned to local parent groups for advice and support. In many cities and towns, parents of children with learning disabilities have formal meetings to help each other. Sometimes parents are more willing to listen to another parent. Some of the more experienced parents will even attend team meetings with you if you need them. Talking to other parents who have been through the system can help you profit from their successes and avoid their mistakes. They will also help you evaluate the services offered to your child and help you make decisions that will influence her educational future.

Parent support groups can also help you learn to trust yourself. One parent said, "The biggest thing that I have learned is to question—even the biggest of professionals. Any theory can stand the test of questioning. Question theories. If they are valid they will hold weight and stand the test of time. Trust your instincts."

In some cases, parents felt the need to hire an outside consultant to help them advocate for their child. These consultants go by many names, and the label you use sets the tone of your meetings. One such specialist told us she prefers to be called an "educational consultant" rather than an "advocate." The term is less threatening to the other members of the team and the mood of the meeting is more relaxed, she said.

Teachers need your support. They are concerned about their students and become uncomfortable when they are treated as adversaries. They worry that parents want them to "fix" their child—to cure the learning disability. Teachers know they have no magic wands to cure your child. They don't have crystal balls either. Your child's teacher cannot predict how long your child will need special services or how successful he will be as an adult. Don't expect a teacher to take on that role.

Teachers want to hear your concerns. It is important for you to voice them, but it is also important to listen to what specialists are saying. One teacher told us it is easier to relate to parents who understand the learning disability and are realistic about it. She felt that parents do a better job if they can separate the child's issues from their own issues.

Teachers get frustrated too. Their frustration is not the same as yours, but it is real. Teachers take their work seriously, and sometimes they feel your child's difficulties reflect on them. Their job is to teach. Your child's job is to learn. When your child is having a problem, they sometimes worry they are not doing their job adequately. That makes them especially sensitive to perceived criticism.

Teachers can get worn down when people criticize them all day, and they might respond in kind. One teacher told us, "People used to yell at me and say they paid my salary and they were going to do what they thought was right. If they didn't get what they wanted, they were going to get their attorney involved. Well, that sort of attack can affect a professional's thinking. The school system has an attorney too. That approach from parents gets very expensive for everyone involved, and often it doesn't resolve the problem."

Unfortunately, some of the parents we talked with felt that, despite their best efforts, they could not get what they wanted through their school system. They looked outside for another opinion.

Not everyone is comfortable with the same things, and you should not feel guilty if you want your child evaluated outside of your local system. However, don't think that just because the evaluation is taking place at a well-known hospital or diagnostic center you don't need to be involved. Involve these diagnosticians as members of your child's educational team just as you would the school team. Work closely with them to make sure you agree with their recommendations.

When looking for a place to seek a second opinion, ask other parents. They are the best source for information about evaluations, teachers, schools, and services.

The team is only as strong as you make it. You can learn a lot from the other team members and they can learn a lot from you.

Chapter 7

Attention Deficit Disorder (ADD) and Attention Deficit Hyperactivity Disorder (ADHD)

Jason demands attention. He spends more time out of his seat than in it. He just can't sit still. His desk is a mess. He interrupts his classmates and his teacher. He wants to talk, not just at appropriate times, but all the time. At recess he runs around by himself. The other children don't understand him, and they don't particularly enjoy being with him. They don't know why he grabs things from them without asking. When he is home sick, his teacher breathes a sigh of relief.

But not his parents. When he is home, their lives are constantly disrupted. His mom can't talk on the phone without being interrupted. She can't feed the baby without having Jason demand more attention. His dad can't take him to the grocery store because Jason pulls things off the shelves. The tables and shelves in their home are bare. Jason bumps into everything and cherished items are destroyed. The only time Jason sits still is when he is playing with his video game. Then, nothing will divert his attention. He won't do his homework, he won't come to the dinner table, he won't get ready for bed. He drives his parents nuts!

If your child has been diagnosed with attention deficit disorder (ADD) or attention deficit hyperactivity disorder (ADHD) he, like Jason, is among the 3 percent of the school-age population with this disorder. Many ADD/ADHD children also have associated learning disabilities, and many exhibit social or emotional problems related to their disabilities. These children have been called lazy, stubborn, willful, rude, obnoxious, disruptive, or simply a pain in the neck.

Jason's parents were actually relieved when they learned he had an attention disorder. It explained his inappropriate behavior. The diagnosis finally took the emphasis away from the punitive and placed it on the positive. Jason's disorder could not be cured, but it could be treated.

The actual diagnosis of ADD or ADHD can only be made by a physician—usually a pediatrician or a neurologist. These professionals make their diagnosis in conjunction with information about your child's behavior at home and at school. Jason's parents were surprised that the physician took less than one hour to examine and observe the boy before confirming his attention deficit problem. Though the actual time spent with Jason was brief, the physician reviewed all information about him, including his strengths, weaknesses, intellectual ability, health, and early developmental history.

The doctor looked for a pattern and for a combination of symptoms reported by Jason's parents, teachers, and other involved professionals over a long period of time. He used the information to rule out other possible reasons for Jason's behavior, including emotional problems, reactions to medications, and allergies.

Jason's behavior was typical for a child with ADHD. In addition to restlessness and overactivity, most ADHD children are easily distracted and need help in controlling their attention. They can exhibit the opposite problem as well: When they find something especially interesting, their attention cannot be diverted. They can involve themselves in a particular activity to the exclusion of all others for long periods of time.

They are often impatient and have trouble waiting their turn. They blurt out answers in the classroom, and they have difficulty following directions. Children with ADHD cannot focus on one thing and are often aware of everything that is going on around them. They shift from one task to another and have difficulty organizing and completing projects. For children with ADHD there is no such thing as quiet play. They talk excessively, interrupt others, and they do not seem to listen. They often misplace things. Because they find it difficult to think before they act, children with ADHD often engage in dangerous activities.

Children with attention deficit disorder without hyperactivity share many of the same problems as children with ADHD. Because their behavior is less outrageous, they are more difficult to identify and are often overlooked.

Rachel never interrupts. She seldom looks up from her paper and won't even make eye contact with her classmates or her teacher. She often gazes out of the window. When there is a lot of activity in the class, she places her head on her desk. She gets lost on her way to gym. Her teacher says she is lazy. Her mother says she isn't trying hard enough. Rachel feels lousy about herself.

ADD children like Rachel are often called stubborn or lazy and are extremely frustrating to their parents and teachers. They share many of the disabilities of an ADHD child, but without the hyperactivity. They might appear to be daydreaming and lost in their imaginations. They rarely finish an activity in the time allowed, and they might ask to have directions repeated over and over—if they allow themselves to try the task at all. Their ability to process and organize information is faulty, and they appear to be out of step with the rest of the family or class. Because these children usually have at least average intelligence, they know something is wrong. Teachers and parents often tell them they need to try harder, but they know they are trying as hard as they can. Children without hyperactivity rarely draw attention to themselves with aggressive behavior or activity, and are often overlooked and become lost once they reach school.

At a recent national conference on ADD, Dr. Edward Hallowell, instructor in psychiatry at Harvard Medical School, explained attention deficits this way: "It's like driving in the rain with bad windshield wipers. Everything is smudged and blurred and you're speeding along, and it's really frustrating not being able to see very well. Or it's like listening to a radio station with a lot of static and you have to strain to hear what's going on. Or it's like trying to build a house of cards in a dust storm. You have to build a structure to protect yourself from the wind before you can even start on the cards.

"In other ways it's like being supercharged all the time. You get one idea and you have to act on it, and then, what do you know, you've got another idea before you've finished up with the first one, and so you go for that one, but of course a third idea intercepts the second, and you just have to follow that one. Pretty soon people are calling you disorganized and impulsive and all sorts of impolite words that miss the point completely. Because you're trying really hard."

I once taught sisters who had learning problems in school. Both girls were very bright and creative, but neither could master the mechanics of phonics or math. Lisa's problem was easy to notice. She was in constant motion with her body as well as her mind. She was always two steps ahead of the teacher at each lesson, and she could not focus on the subject at hand.

Her sister, Diane, was more of a puzzle. She was never a behavior problem in class. Instead, she sat quietly and gazed off into space. She could not maintain eye contact with the teacher, and she had difficulty keeping her attention on the lesson on the board. In situations where she was expected to work independently in a quiet area, she would spend the entire time staring at one problem or exercise on her paper. It took her teachers longer to realize that Diane was as distractible and inattentive as Lisa. Lisa is hyperactive and has been diagnosed with ADHD. Her sister has attention deficit disorder, but she is not hyperactive. Once their learning disabilities were identified and treated, both were able to learn. As they got older, they found ways of channeling their learning styles into activities that made them feel successful. Diane enjoyed acting in high school, and Lisa excelled at playing the drums with a rock band.

Children with ADD and with ADHD share another common problem: They usually have difficulty making or keeping friends. They are smart enough to know they are not doing what other children in class can do with ease. They are often yelled at for being disruptive or for not participating.

One psychologist who works with ADD children told us self-esteem is a real problem for children with ADD and ADHD. One of her young patients is typical. He said he could make friends, but he couldn't keep them. His inattentive behavior caused him to wet his pants and he was ridiculed by his classmates. She acknowledged many ADD and ADHD children are difficult to like. They interrupt, they don't listen, they are impulsive, they distract their classmates, and they are at their worst in a school situation with many sources of stimulation, she said.

Because they respond best in one-to-one situations, they are often removed from their classmates to special resource rooms for remediation. This may help with their academic skills, but it further isolates them from their classmates. Those who are singled out and sent to a special remedial class are sometimes teased and ridiculed. No wonder their self-esteem is so low.

Family life suffers when children have ADHD. Nights out are impossible for parents. Uninformed baby sitters won't come back. When parents take children along, their evening is disrupted.

Much as they hate to admit it, parents often find children with ADD and especially ADHD difficult. They love their children, but often they don't *like* them. And that's not surprising; these children are very difficult to be with.

Specialists have not come to agreement on causes for ADD or ADHD, and different treatments have been recommended over the years. Children have been treated with special diets, eye muscle exercises, and megavitamins. Anecdotal information indicates some of these methods have been successful for some children.

Current treatment for ADD and ADHD involves stimulant medications such as Ritalin, Cylert, or Dexedrine in combination with tutoring and counseling. Many medical professionals believe children with attention disorders don't have enough neuro-transmitter—a chemical in the brain. The result is that their brains are like a TV set that is out of focus. All of the signals are there—they're just not in the right combination. These drugs temporarily increase the supply of neuro-transmitter, allowing the brain to work in proper sequence. Many parents are afraid of such drugs, and that fear often keeps them from seeking help for their child. They are frightened about drugs in general and worry that their child will become addicted. When medication is recommended for asthma or diabetes, parents seem to accept the idea that their child will be dependent on a drug in order to lead a normal life. But when the drug can alter the child's behavior, parents worry they may be giving the child drugs to make their own lives easier. Many feel they have failed as parents if their child must be drugged to be "normal." Those parents who have found that drug therapy improved their child's quality of life said they wondered why they didn't do it sooner.

These drugs, however, are not without side effects. Some children experience a loss of appetite. Others have difficulty sleeping. Some studies have documented involuntary movements and depression. Current studies indicate these problems are not long lasting, but the effects of unmedicated ADD and ADHD may be. The damage to your child's self-esteem as well as the damage to the quality of life for your family can have long-term effects.

Drug therapy has been beneficial for many children. One student explained that when he took the medication he could still hear his friends outside the classroom, but he was able to tune out their voices and pay attention to his work.

Drugs will not cure attention problems, but when properly supervised, they have proven to be very effective in helping many children filter out unimportant stimulation in order to concentrate. Many believe the results are worth it.

According to Atlanta pediatrician Dr. Michael K. Levine, "ADHD is most effectively treated with a combination of approaches and therapies. These can include behavior modification, tutoring, counseling, involvement of the pediatrican and the family with the school as a support system for the child, and finally, medication.

"Not all children should be treated with medication. There are many children with ADHD who don't need medication. To find out which ones would benefit, the first step is to have them examined by their physician to see if some other medical problem is causing the hyperactive behavior," says Levine. A routine exam can eliminate other medical causes for hyperactive behavior, such as a hearing deficit or elevated lead levels in the blood. If no medical problems causing the ADHD are found, then a trial of medication might be considered.

With the support of family, physicians, and teachers, the positive side of ADD and ADHD has a chance to emerge. ADD and ADHD children have a unique way of looking at things. They absorb much more of the world around them than those with "normal" attention spans. With their special vision, they often succeed in the creative arts. Maybe your child will create an artistic masterpiece or write the great American novel. As he jumps from idea to idea, he may be the one to discover a cure for cancer.

An effective team approach can help your child to channel the energy, curiosity, and focus that are associated with attention deficits into positive activities.

With treatment, "the child who has been reprimanded for

blurting something out, is then praised for having blurted out something brilliant," says Hallowell. So join the team and begin celebrating your child's individuality.

What You Can Do at Home

Most parents we spoke to said their family lives improved when their ADD or ADHD child received supervised treatment in combination with a stimulant medication. They were quick to add, however, that drug treatment alone is not enough.

The demands on a family with a ADD or ADHD child are enormous. Children with ADD and ADHD need organized, patient, tireless parents to help them stay focused during daily activities, both at home and at school. Parents suggested strategies for making what can sometimes seem an overwhelming experience more tolerable.

Talk with your child about his learning disability. Be frank and encourage him to talk openly about the difficulties the attention deficit causes. Work together on strategies to help compensate for the problem.

Children with attention deficit disorders need more structure in all tasks. Tell them or show them exactly what you want them to do. If you want them to set the table, show them exactly what they need to put on the table and where each item goes. It may be necessary to repeat the demonstration many times before it becomes a pattern for the child.

Whenever you are talking to your child, make sure you have her attention. Make solid eye contact. Have your child repeat your instructions, and encourage her to ask questions if she does not understand.

Give the child ample time to complete a task and to prepare for the next event. Children without attention deficit can switch gears with little problem, but a child with ADD or ADHD needs more time to prepare for a change in activity. He needs cues. If he is playing with his toys and it is almost time for dinner, don't wait until the last minute to call the child to the table. About 15 minutes before dinner, say, "We will be eating dinner in 15 minutes. Start putting your toys away."

Provide your child with clear expectations. Subtleties are lost on a child with attention deficit. Explain that if he picks up his toys before your guests arrive, you will have time to read him a story. If cleanup takes too long, there will be no time for reading.

ADD children perform best when their tasks are performed according to a routine with as little variation as possible. For example, if your child is responsible for feeding the goldfish, feeding time should always follow the same schedule—just before dinner, for example, or right after breakfast. Provide another activity that triggers a reminder for the child.

Scheduling charts help children anticipate upcoming activities. For those with reading difficulties, try cutting out pictures related to daily events and place them where the child can review them. These visual reminders help children with attention deficit prepare for their activities.

Children with ADHD have energy levels that often leave their parents wilting with fatigue. Schedule a regular time for high-energy activities. Some parents enjoy using this time with their child. They feel that the shared activity helps strengthen their relationship. Other parents enroll their children in group exercise activities. Though not all children with attention deficits thrive in organized sports, many do. Some parents use their child's activity time for much-needed relaxation.

Be realistic in your expectations. Though the show at the science center may offer a wealth of information for your child, if he can't sit through it, he won't learn anything and you will only become more frustrated.

One of the saddest things about ADD and ADHD is the way it affects children's social lives. Because they have difficulty communicating, it is often hard for them to make and to keep friends. Watching children with attention deficit interact with their peers is often difficult for parents.

Sometimes parents try to compensate for their child's lack of social skills by trying to "buy" friends for their children. They may invite the entire class for a bowling party or other special event in an effort to foster friendships for the child. This sort of behavior can actually backfire. Children know when their social skills are less than adequate and your child may feel less competent if you "need" to invite large groups of friends.

Instead, invite one child. Encourage the children to work at tasks they can accomplish in order to develop your child's self-confidence. Your child might be good at building with large blocks for example, or finger painting, soccer skills, musical activities, videos, play acting, or swimming. The key is to keep the activities simple and short.

Most parents work hard to understand and to accommodate their child's learning disability, but that doesn't make conflicts disappear. Discipline is often an issue. Every parent we spoke to stressed that discipline must be consistent. It is important for mothers and fathers to agree on consequences and to administer them in a predictable way.

Many ADD and ADHD children do not have the ability to understand the action/consequence relationship. If they cannot comprehend how one action led to another, punishment has no value. When your child acts inappropriately, take the time to explain appropriate alternatives. For example, if your child grabs another child's toy, explain that he should have asked for the toy rather than pulling it away. Rather than punishing for poor behavior, praise good behavior. That reinforces the child's good behavior without overemphasizing the negative actions.

Sometimes parents can't do it alone. More than one parent confessed that it was difficult to react positively to a child with an attention deficit. Many said they love their children, but sometimes they really don't like them. Don't feel guilty. Children with attention deficits can provoke the most loving and dedicated parents into short tempers.

Many people can be a source of help. Choose your child's pediatrician carefully. Make sure you ask the right questions in order to find a doctor who is comfortable working with you and your child. Ask other parents of children with ADD and ADHD for a recommendation. When you make an appointment with the doctor, ask about his or her interest and experience in working with children with learning disabilities. Ask how the doctor handles children with ADD and ADHD. Make sure you like the doctor's answers.

Energetic baby-sitters can give parents a much-needed break. Parents who can schedule one-to-one time with their children find it very rewarding. A baby-sitter who has not yet developed the necessary skills to supervise your ADD/ADHD child could watch his brothers or sisters while the two of you share a special activity. Sometimes it is helpful for one parent to stay at home with the other children while the other shares a special time with the attention deficit youngster. When these special times are scheduled into your week, it provides your child with structure and gives him something to look forward to.

Though ADD and ADHD children often have trouble interacting with other children or in small groups, they flourish in the company of a caring adult. Grandparents often have special relationships with these children. If you are fortunate enough to have grandparents close by, let them help.

Many of the parents we spoke to said they get up very early in the morning in order to have some time for themselves—for reading, for exercise, for extended conversations with their spouses. They also go to bed early. Parenting a child with an attention deficit disorder is a high-energy occupation, and adequate rest is essential.

It can be frustrating, it can be maddening, but it can also be very rewarding. Without these high-energy kids, life would be so dull!

Chapter 8

Language Disabilities

The family was sitting around the dinner table having an animated conversation about their day at the zoo. Seven-year-old Ethan scratched his ribs and said, "Did you see those monkeys picking bugs off each other?"

"Yeah," said his little brother, giggling. "And they ate them too."

"Do you think the polar bears live at the zoo in the summer?" Ethan asked.

Their parents laughed as the dinner conversation continued, but they were concerned. Their daughter, Laurie, had added nothing to the conversation. Though she seemed to have had a wonderful time exploring at the zoo, she sat quietly at the table. She was not able to share her experiences.

Laurie has a learning disability in the area of communication.

Communication is our most human characteristic. Without the ability to communicate, your child, like Laurie, might have trouble sharing her thoughts. Without strong communication skills, she might have trouble participating in the classroom and getting along in social situations as well.

If your child has a communication disorder, she might also have trouble understanding what she hears or reads. This makes it difficult for her to learn from you, from her teachers, from books at school, and from everything else that goes on around her.

When schools talk about communication, they usually refer to it as "speech and language" in the same breath—the speech and language teacher, the speech and language class, the speech and language evaluation. But the communication of language is different from the communication of speech. Speech is the *how* of what we say; language is *what* we say. If your child has a speech problem, you are aware of it every time he speaks. If your child has a language problem, it is not always as obvious.

If your child exhibits more than several of the following behaviors, he may have a disability in the area of language:

Has your child had recurring ear infections?

Has his hearing ever been impaired? Does he turn up the volume on the TV?

Does she frequently ask to have information repeated?

Does she misunderstand directions?

Does he forget what you have told him to do?

Does he remember part of your instructions but not all of them?

Does she have a hard time paying attention when there is other noise?

Does he have trouble expressing himself?

Does he use incorrect grammar beyond an appropriate age?

Is she having trouble with schoolwork?

Does he prefer to play alone?

If you can answer yes to several of these questions, read on. A better understanding of language will help you understand a language disability.

There are two areas of language: the language of understanding what we hear or read, *receptive,* and the language of saying and writing what we want others to hear or read, *expressive.* Both receptive and expressive language involve the proper use of words and their meanings as well as an understanding of and the ability to use correct grammar.

Simply put, language is a code or collection of symbols where words are used to represent things and ideas. We know a *car* is a vehicle we get into and it takes us places. *Hungry* is what we feel when our stomachs make noises and we want something to eat. In addition to the symbols, language also has rules that must be followed in order for people to communicate with each other effectively. One reason we find it so difficult to communicate with people from other countries is because their language codes and rules are not the same as ours.

The English language rules tell us that more than one child is "children" and that the sentence "Children hurt" has a different meaning than "Hurt children." It is okay for your child to tell you, "I want something to eat," but you would probably be very embarrassed if he said the same thing to a stranger. Children with difficulties in language may have trouble making these types of distinctions. For a child with language disabilities, words, phrases, and sentences are often confused or misused.

Children use receptive language skills to follow a spoken or written direction and to understand what the teacher says in class, what they read in a book, or watch on television.

Some children with receptive language difficulties have had ear infections or problems with their hearing, but many have never had ear problems. The diagnosis is not that simple. A child with language difficulties can have perfect hearing. All sounds get into his brain without interference. It is what happens to the information once it is in there that causes problems. Once information gets into the brain, it must be recognized, analyzed, organized, memorized, and recalled. Specialists call this processing what is heard. A breakdown in any one of these processes can result in language difficulties for your child.

Whew! It sounds complicated because it is. All of these processes must work well, they must work together, and they must work at the right time. And they must work *all* of the time. One of the most frustrating aspects of a receptive language disability is that your child might seem to understand something one day, and the next day she seems to have no clue. This is more often the rule than the exception.

"This kid is a space shot," the coach told the assistant. "I told him to take the field, and he looked at me with this blank stare. He's supposed to be playing left field. We've played six games this season, and he still doesn't know where to go."

Johnny isn't a "space shot," he has a receptive language disability. His inability to follow directions is not based on stupidity or on defiance, but on a gap in his abilities.

Many children with language disabilities have difficulty with abstract language. What does "take the field" mean anyway? Johnny may be busy thinking, "How can I *take* the field?" Last week his coach told him to stand near the sign on the fence, and he had no trouble understanding where to go. In the coach's mind "go stand by the sign" and "take the field" mean the same thing. For Johnny, they are not even in the same ballpark!

Sometimes children have little difficulty in the area of receptive language but, like Laurie, they have difficulties expressing themselves. Children use expressive language when they participate in a conversation, answer a question, tell a story, describe an event or object, or write anything.

Children who have difficulty expressing themselves might appear to be less intelligent, because we tend to judge a person's ability by how well he expresses himself.

Three-year-old Tara had not started to speak—not a word. Her mother was very concerned and took her to a local hospital for evaluation. "She's retarded," the specialist told Tara's mother.

"She's not retarded," the mother responded. "She understands what I say. She does what I tell her to. She just doesn't speak," the mother said in tears.

Fortunately, Tara's mother trusted her instincts. She took her daughter to a language pathologist. The news was much better. Tara had a severe expressive language delay. Following several years of language therapy, she is a happy typical sixth-grade student.

Tara's mother suspected that intelligence and verbal expression are not necessarily related, and she was right.

Intelligence tests often rely heavily on expressive language skills. Tara's IQ score came out low because she did not have the skills necessary to do well on the test, not because of a lack of intelligence.

Expressive language is complicated because everything that comes in must then get out. Sometimes your child knows what he is talking about, but the words come out wrong or not at all.

One of the parents we talked to explained, "Jon knows the word 'brown,' but if someone asks him, 'What color is that dog?' he will search for the word that means that color. He might have trouble finding the correct word."

Another child, Barbara, can name every letter in the alphabet, but when her teacher shows her the letter *B* and asks her to name it, she can't.

Susan, a high school student, took her friends for a ride in her car. She told them all to be sure to fasten their life jackets. She meant to tell them to fasten their seat belts, but somehow the other words came out.

Susan, Barbara, and Jon have word retrieval problems. They are not always able to call up the right word at the right time. In adults we often refer to these misstatements as "Freudian slips."

Sometimes expressive language problems contribute to behavioral problems. Many temper tantrums are the result of a child's inability to use language to make himself understood.

When Amy's homework was too hard, her mother said Amy would yell, "This is stupid!" and throw her books on the floor. Fights often erupted between Amy and her father, and Amy would end up losing her television time. After Amy's expressive language problem was diagnosed and her parents were encouraged to help Amy use words to express her frustration, family life became much calmer.

Some parents told us their language-delayed children speak so slowly that the other children in the family don't give them time to get their thoughts out. In the home, as well as in school, the child who talks the fastest is often the one who ends up speaking the most. We are not always sure what the other children in the family or class know or want to say, because they are not allowed time to gather their thoughts together and get them out.

Many children with expressive language disabilities also have problems with written expression. The written part of expressive language requires your child to use all of her oral language skills in combination with her ability to write and to use correct grammar. No wonder many of these children hate to write anything down!

Children can have either expressive or receptive language delays, and they may also have a combination of both. When the information they receive is faulty, the information they give back will usually be incorrect as well.

Though most of us think of listening and speaking when we think of language and communication, there is another communication area that can present difficulties for children: understanding and using appropriate body language. One parent told us a story that illustrates the problems resulting from this type of disability.

"I was escorting my son upstairs to his room," she said. "I was furious with him. He had been misbehaving all morning, and I was at my wit's end. I was scowling as I marched him up the steps. Instead of seeing by my facial expression that I was upset, he looked at me and laughed and said, 'You have a curler in your hair.' He just could not read my anger through my facial expression."

This type of inability is typical of children with body language difficulties. Think about how often we use this skill every day. We know just by looking at their faces when our friends are happy to see us. We also know when we have interrupted a confrontation between two people without ever hearing what they said to each other. Without even having to ask, we know our children are upset when we see them with their heads and shoulders drooping.

Imagine what it would be like not to be able to read those silent signals. A child who can read body language knows his dad is angry with his behavior by simply looking at the way his father stands and the expression on his face. The father expects his child to respond in a certain way when the child sees he is angry. A child with body language difficulties never gets the message. His father must tell the child with words, not actions, how he is feeling. He would have to say, "I am very upset about the way you behaved just now, and I expect you to apologize for what you have done."

It is not hard to imagine the types of problems a child with a body language disability might encounter in social situations. Much of what goes on at a school playground is done without spoken language. Children interact with each other with signs and symbols, and children with this disability either cannot read them at all, or they misunderstand the message. When they try to mimic the body language they see, they often get themselves into even more trouble.

When a child taps another child on the shoulder to get his attention, the other child usually turns around, smiles, and waits to hear what the other child wants. A child without the ability to express these subtleties might punch another child in the shoulder to get his attention. When the other child responds with anger instead of a smile, the child with a body language disability doesn't understand what he did wrong.

The specific characteristics of children who have language difficulties are as different as the children themselves. If your child has a language problem, it is probably unlike that of the language-delayed child next door. If you have concerns in any of these areas, have your child evaluated by a speech and language specialist (sometimes called a speech and language therapist or pathologist) at your child's school. The specialist will administer a variety of tests to help pinpoint specific areas of strength and weakness. If the tests determine your child needs therapy, professionals at your school will help strengthen weaknesses with specific language therapy. If necessary, specialists will provide the classroom teacher with specific strategies to make sure your child learns in spite of any language problem. For more information about specific language tests, see Chapter 13.

What Can You Do at Home

There are many things you can do at home to provide a language-rich environment for your child.

Read to your child. When you do so, you can expand his vocabulary and his listening skills in a nonteaching, nurturing environment. This helps develop both your child's receptive and expressive language skills.

Be a solid role model for your child and don't talk down to her. Don't say, "We're going to the tooth doctor." How is the child going to learn the word "dentist" if he doesn't hear you use it? Say instead, "We're going to the dentist. She is a doctor for your teeth." Avoid following up your explanation with a quiz. Often parents will say, "We're going to the aquarium. That's a place where we will see fish. Now tell me, what is an aquarium?" Remember, you are the parent, not the teacher.

Children learn most skills by mimicking. Don't be afraid to use adult words when talking to your child. This is a way to encourage his curiosity about language and to expand his vocabulary. If your child uses inappropriate language structure, rather than correcting his language, repeat the sentence in the correct way. For example, if Max says, "Max no like broccoli," say back to him, "Oh, Max doesn't like broccoli."

Expose your children to language opportunities, and talk to them. When you go to the beach, talk about the different types of shells you see. Look for opportunities to talk about the different animals and fish living in the ocean or pond. Talk about the kinds of creatures they will find in the sea and what kinds of creatures they will find on land. When you walk through your neighborhood, notice the different colors and shapes of cars parked along the road. Talk about the differences in the way people dress, their sizes, or their ages.

Show that language is valued by encouraging your child to talk even if her language is faulty. Encourage your child to tell you about her day or about a favorite television program. If your child wants to talk, listen. Children often pick their parents' busiest time to share their thoughts. When possible, slow down and take time to listen. It might be necessary to ask the more talkative siblings to slow down their responses so your language-delayed child has a chance to understand a conversation and contribute.

Make up games that will build vocabulary. Play 20 questions and word games. Ask your child questions that require more than a one- or two-word response. Rather than asking, "Did you have fun in school today?" say, "Tell me what happened at recess today."

Encourage your child to talk, and take time to listen. Those two things are the most effective in encouraging language development.

Help your child with word retrieval and word memory skills by playing memory games. Use mnemonic devices to connect new information to something she already knows. We used these tricks when we were kids. Remember how we recalled the names of the Great Lakes (Huron, Ontario, Michigan, Erie, and Superior) by the word HOMES? Similar tricks can help your child.

Take your child grocery shopping. The grocery store is an area rich in language and expressions.

When giving directions to your child, make sure the directions are logical and simple. Use words like *first, next, last,* to help him organize. If you are not sure he understands, ask him to repeat what you have said. Use pictures and demonstrations where possible. You can make picture charts of routine chores so he can refer back to the chart if he forgets the steps involved in each task.

If you are aware your child has difficulties with body language, you may need to emphasize the importance of facial expression. If you are angry, say, "Look at my face. This is an angry face." If the child punches you to get your attention, stop and explain that punching is inappropriate. Show him how you would like him to get your attention. Sometimes children need outside counseling to help them understand why they are having difficulty in social situations.

Don't be discouraged. Language disabilities are complicated, but with treatment and patience, language skills can be strengthened.

Chapter 9

Speech Disabilities

It was Tiona's turn to talk about her stuffed animal. Students in her second grade class were gathered in a circle to share information about their favorite animal. After sharing information, they were to write a paragraph about their toy pet.

Tiona reluctantly began her description. She hadn't made it through her first sentence before one of her classmates started laughing and said, "She sounds like Elmer Fudd."

Though his comments were unkind, he was right. Tiona called her stuffed bunny a *wabbit.* She said he was *weely* soft and *bwown.* His favorite food is *owange cawwots,* she said.

Tiona's parents thought her speech was cute. Until they got a phone call from her teacher, they didn't realize how much her speech disability was affecting her academic and social life. Because the children often laughed at her when she spoke, Tiona was quiet. Even during recess, she was hesitant to carry on conversations with her classmates. She was embarrassed by her speech.

Tiona was slightly late in developing her *r* sounds. The real indication that she needed help, however, was that she felt uncomfortable about her speech. For speech specialists, this is often one of the important factors in determining if a child should receive speech services.

Speech is an essential component in a child's academic development. In order to develop their language and reading skills, children need practice in speaking and reading aloud. Oral expression is the most common form of communication in the early grades.

When children express themselves in school, speech difficulties may become obvious. Children with problems in the area of speech do not necessarily have trouble expressing themselves. Speech creates a problem only because others have trouble understanding or because others laugh at faulty speech patterns.

While speech difficulties are often obvious to teachers and others in school, parents are sometimes the last to recognize the difficulty. Parents may become so accustomed to their child's speech pattern that they have no difficulty understanding what the child is saying. Sometimes they are surprised to learn others have trouble understanding their child.

One parent we spoke to told us she did not realize her son's speech problem was interfering with his classroom activity until she got a call from his teacher. The mother could understand him, but his teacher and classmates couldn't.

Speech problems include difficulty in articulation, that is, in pronouncing the sounds in words; problems with fluency such as stuttering; and voice disorders (such as hoarseness or monotone).

Problems with articulation can have different causes, and in this case the cause is important, because it affects the method used to correct the problem. Sometimes students who have suffered recurring ear infections also suffer reduced hearing. An intermittent hearing loss puts these children at risk for developing speech problems. If children cannot hear sounds properly, they will not learn to say them correctly.

The muscles of the mouth, tongue, and palate help children form the proper sounds. When children have difficulties coordinating these muscles, they have trouble forming the shapes that produce the sounds. For example, *R*'s might come out sounding like *W*'s. *S*'s may sound like *Z*'s. *Th* sounds may come out sounding like *D*'s. Final sounds may not come out at all: land becomes *lan,* fork becomes *for*. Beginning sounds can also cause a problem; a child might say *poon* instead of spoon or *tar* instead of star.

In order for the tongue and lips to produce the proper sounds, they must first receive the correct message from the brain. When the muscles of the mouth don't work properly, or when the mental message is short-circuited, speech is difficult.

Sometimes a student has adequate musculature but continues to speak improperly because he has learned an incorrect pattern. These habits must be corrected without damaging a child's self-esteem or his enthusiasm for talking.

What parents call "baby talk" is cute in a toddler, but is not appropriate once a child enters school. Just as there are guidelines for language development, there are developmental stages in speech development. These general guidelines are often used as one basis for determining whether a speech difficulty interferes with learning.

Around the age of two months, babies begin to babble. After six months, they combine vowels and consonants to form words such as "ma" and "da."

Between 8 and 12 months, they copy sounds they hear and combine syllables, such as "da-da" and "ma-ma." The length and number of words increase as the child gets older.

By the age of three, the typical child's speech is 90 to 100 percent intelligible. Certain sounds may not be perfect but are still within the normal range. Later developing sounds include *t, g, sh,* and *ch*. Other sounds develop still later: *z, s, v, r,* and *th*.

Some children do not have problems with articulation, but have trouble with the rhythm of their speech. Stuttering is the involuntary repetition, lengthening, or blockage of a word or part of a word. Sometimes these disabilities are referred to as fluency problems.

Approximately 5 percent of all children stutter for several months or more during their lives. Many of them stop within a year. Stuttering occurs more often in some situations than others. It is more common in situations where children are excited or tired. Stuttering is unpredictable and confuses even the experts. No one knows for certain why children stutter, but there are some things we do know.

About three times as many boys as girls stutter. Most children who stutter begin before they are 5 years old. It is very rare for this type of speech pattern to begin after age 12. Despite popular myth, children who stutter are no more anxious than children who don't.

Stuttering becomes a problem in school because children are forced into situations where they need to communicate through speech. The disability can prevent a child from succeeding in areas where he is quite capable.

Untreated, stuttering can result in poorly developed social skills. Children who stutter have difficulty carrying on conversations and speaking in class. They are embarrassed and are often ridiculed for their speech disability. Most of us can remember a child in our class who stuttered and those agonizing moments when other children laughed as he tried to speak.

If after the age of 30 months a child stutters for more than 6 months and in more than one situation, it is important to have him evaluated.

Difficulties with voice may stem from overuse or abuse—persistent shouting, screaming, or squealing can contribute to the problem. Children with voice problems have difficulty controlling their voice production. They may speak too loudly, or softly, or in a monotone. Their pitch might be too high or too low, or the quality might be hoarse or breathy. Children who are shouting may have a hearing loss. Those who speak softly may not be shy; they may have damaged vocal cords.

Children with chronic difficulties in any of these three areas of speech should be evaluated. Your child will need to have a complete hearing test to eliminate hearing difficulties as a source of the problem. Most often these are scheduled with an audiologist recommended by your child's pediatrician.

Once hearing difficulties have been ruled out as the source of the problem, speech and language professionals will administer tests to help determine the specific cause of the speech difficulty. These professionals will develop your child's educational plan based on the results of the tests. A listing of specific speech and language tests is included in Chapter 13.

If speech therapy is recommended, specialists at your child's school will provide it as part of your child's special education program.

As with most disabilities, a speech problem can create issues with self-esteem. Specialists are sensitive to these emotional needs, but parents need to help in this area as well. Understand that your child may be embarrassed by his speech, and validate his feelings. Encourage him to speak, and praise him for what he says even if you are not yet able to praise him for the quality of his speech production. Tell him his speech will improve with practice. If you cannot understand what your child is saying, tell him you are having difficulty hearing and he may need to repeat what he says. Occasionally, despite repetition, you will not be able to understand what your child is saying. Don't expect to understand every word. Usually the meaning can be determined by the context of the situation.

If your child stutters, allow him to finish his sentences. Though it may be frustrating, try as much as possible not to interrupt the flow of his ideas. Respond to what he says, not how he says it.

Talk with your friends and family about the way you treat your child's stuttering, and encourage them to respond in the same way.

If your child stutters, it is important for you to speak in a less hurried pace when talking to him. You can become a model of correct speech patterns. When you take a less hurried approach, it serves to slow things down and encourages your child to speak more slowly. When your child uses an incorrect form of speech, repeat the word in the proper form. For example, if he says, "My teacher read *da dree* little pigs today," say back to him, "Did you enjoy the story of *the three* little pigs?" If he stutters and says, "I w-w-w-want my c-c-c-cookie now," repeat the words your child uses, "Oh, you want your cookie now," to provide a correct model. If your child needs to work on his voice production, be sure you vary your pitch, volume, and tone as an example.

Turn off the television, especially during mealtimes. The more opportunities you provide for conversation, the more your child will be able to practice his skills.

Most importantly, let your child know you believe what he says is as important as how he says it. Value his ideas and encourage him to express them.

Chapter 10

Reading Disabilities—Dyslexia

Whenever Sherry read to her six-year-old son, David, he loved it. He would snuggle up to her and hang on her every word. He loved to hear stories, but he also enjoyed articles from children's magazines about plant and animal life, especially the ones about dinosaurs. He would talk for hours about what he heard.

Story times were his favorite part of the day. That was one of the reasons Sherry was so surprised that David showed no interest in the words in the books she was reading. His older brother had enjoyed the prereading activities presented on "Sesame Street," but David always found something else to do when she tuned into the program.

In fact, David did not like doing anything visual. He hated doing puzzles and even looked like he was in pain when he tried to put Lego pieces together. He would rather play outside in the rain than take part in what his family considered rainy-day activities.

When Sherry talked to David's first grade teacher about his preferences, the teacher dismissed her as an overly anxious mother. Because David's brother was bright and advanced for his age in school, the teacher implied that Sherry was comparing the two boys. "Perhaps he just isn't as gifted as his older brother," the teacher said. Sherry had trouble accepting that. She knew David was every bit as bright as his older brother. He just wasn't developing his skills as quickly.

When it was clear that David was not learning to read at the same rate as the other students in his class, Sherry was reluctant to mention it again. She figured that the teacher was the authority and must know much more than Sherry did—after all, she was only a mother.

By the end of first grade David knew the sounds of the consonants but did not know any vowel sounds. He knew a few words by sight, but only the ones that were used over and over again in school. He still carried on knowledgeable conversations at home about topics he heard about or learned by being read to.

But he hated school. He was extremely frustrated by everything there and was only happy when he was playing with his trucks or running around outside. Sherry finally pushed her reluctance aside and insisted that David be evaluated.

Lucky for David that she did. Testing showed that he was extremely bright (Sherry knew that), but that he had severe problems in understanding and remembering what he saw. He also had difficulty organizing his work. The tests revealed problems with visual perception, memory, and organization that caused him to have difficulty learning to read. Many school systems and diagnostic centers refer to this combination of learning disabilities as dyslexia.

There are almost as many definitions of dyslexia as there are diagnostic centers. Current research indicates that dyslexia is a neurological disorder that causes delays in acquiring written language skills, specifically in the area of reading and spelling. Because the term "dyslexic" is so commonly used by professionals and parents to identify children who have trouble learning to read, we have used the term in this chapter. Parents should be aware, however, that many school systems use other terminology to define this type of learning disability.

Learning disability specialists across the country continue to look for answers regarding dyslexia and associated reading disabilities. Experts are looking for causes and cures every day; new theories and teaching methods are announced regularly. Though it is comforting to know that professionals are continually reviewing findings in the area, most parents are more eager to know what they can do right now to help their child. To get started, it is important to learn your child's strengths and weaknesses and work with your school's professionals to develop a strategy to help teach him to read.

Your child's strengths and weaknesses can best be identified through an evaluation by your school's special education professionals. In some school systems, the evaluation is administered by the special needs teachers. In other systems, school psychologists do the testing.

If evaluations determine your child has a reading problem, it is important to understand that it is not the end of the world. Woodrow Wilson was dyslexic. Auguste Rodin and Hans Christian Andersen had dyslexia, and many suspect Edison, Einstein, and Da Vinci had dyslexia as well. Their lives were not hindered by the learning disability. In fact, they were probably enriched because of it. They may have seen the world differently from the rest of us and used their creative talents to communicate in their own way. Our lives are enriched by their creativity also.

A reading problem may be caused by a variety of factors. Just as no two students are alike, no two reading problems are exactly the same. Remediation needs to be specialized and tailored to each students particular learning style.

Julie, a third grade student, cannot remember what she reads long enough for her to make sense of an entire paragraph. It takes her so long to sound out the word "bird" that she forgets the rest of the sentence.

Shira, a first grader, can't see the differences between certain letters in words. She confuses *m* and *n*, and *d* and *b*. "The doy ran with his bog" doesn't make any sense to her.

Another student has difficulty understanding what he reads

because he doesn't understand what the words used in science and social studies classes mean. The idea of *continent* and *mineral* are just too abstract.

Still another student can't keep his attention on the lesson long enough to understand what he needs to know. He doesn't have any of the problems that the other students have, but he can't focus on his reading lesson.

No one program of remediation could help all these students. Each needs a program designed specifically for his or her particular learning style.

In order to better understand your child's particular reading disability, it helps to get some idea of how the reading process works. We can compare the working of the brain to that of a computer. First, information must get inside. In reading, that information gets in through vision. After the words are inside, they must be converted into meanings and ideas. This is where the computer's memory takes over. The words and ideas must stay in the working brain long enough to be of use. If what your child sees is faulty, the information that gets into her computer is incorrect. If Shira sees *dog* as *bog*, it is *bog* that will get into the computer.

As more items are stored in your child's memory bank, she increases the number of clues she will have to help her make sense of the unknown. If Shira doesn't know that a bog is a swamp, she doesn't have the clues she needs to decipher the sentence and recognize that it doesn't make sense. Things aren't much easier for Shira if she knows the meaning of the word, but at least she knows she has made a mistake and searches for a word that will fit the context of the sentence. She's smart. Often she is able to call up the word that fits in the sentence.

Whew! Okay, she has the words in her computer, the memory is working, and the sentence begins to make sense. Now Shira has to hold onto the meaning of that sentence long enough to combine it with the rest of the sentences in the paragraph. What makes learning disabilities so frustrating and complex is their inconsistency.

Sometimes the information might make perfect sense to Shira and she will respond in such a way that you know she understood what she read or heard. The next day—or the next minute—the same information may appear to be meaningless to her. And that's just one child's way of seeing things. The other children we mentioned have different reasons for their reading difficulties.

Children with disabilities in the area of reading might have trouble taking in the information, they might have trouble using the information once it is stored, or they may have trouble getting the information out. A remediation program can only be successful when it is geared to the specific area or areas of need. The diagnosis of a reading problem involves determining where the difficulty lies. That is why a thorough diagnostic evaluation is so important.

A complete reading evaluation will look at your child's ability to recognize (discriminate), remember, and understand (process) information taken in through seeing. Vision problems that are medical in nature are not assessed in a reading evaluation, and this possibly should be investigated before academic testing begins. It is misleading to test how your child sees the printed words if he has difficulty seeing.

The test will determine whether your child can see and hear likenesses and differences in letters, words, and sounds. A *d* must be seen and heard as different from a *b*. The word *saw* must be seen as different from the word *was*. A listing of some of these tests can be found in Chapter 13.

Though a child may have no difficulty hearing differences, he might have trouble seeing differences. Many children with disabilities in this area have problems with reversals or transpositions. Children with reversal difficulties may confuse *b*'s and *d*'s, *p*'s and *q*'s, *6*'s and *9*'s, for example. When they look at the word *saw*, they might see *was*. *On* becomes *no*.

Those with transposition difficulties might see *girl* instead of *grill* or they might see the word *bird* and say *brid*.

Those with difficulty in hearing similarities and differences might not recognize that *bear* and *care* rhyme. They might not be able to recognize that *ball* and *boy* have the same beginning sound.

A test of auditory and visual discrimination will examine how your child sees and hears letters and words and whether his developmental level in these skills is appropriate for his age.

An evaluation might also determine your child's ability to distinguish letters and pictures from the background in which they appear. The letters of a word in a book can "run together" for your child in a way that prevents her from making sense of them. A child with difficulties in this area might frequently lose her place when reading or copying from the board or from a book. She might become confused by pages that have a lot of words on them. Puzzles, picture books, mazes and many other activities that we usually think of as fun for children can actually frustrate those with problems in this area.

An evaluation of memory involves seeing if your child can remember what was seen or heard long enough to use it. He needs to use short-term memory—what he remembers as long as he is paying attention to it—and long-term memory—what remains stored in his brain to be used later. Learning to read relies heavily on memory. Your child is expected to remember the names of the 26 letters of the alphabet, the different sounds they can make, the sounds they make when a few of them are combined (blends), and the words they make when all of the sounds are put together. They also need to remember what these words mean.

Your child must remember the visual picture of the word, be able to see how one word differs from another, and associate that visual picture with the correct sound or sounds for that word. If you compare this to your trying to learn a foreign language, you might begin to wonder how anyone learns to read at all! A thorough evaluation will let you know if your child's memory skills are appropriately developed for his age.

The evaluation will also include an examination of your child's processing skills. It will look at how your child uses everything he has already learned in order to make sense of any new information.

Knowing how *bear* sounds can help him pronounce the word *wear*. Understanding the habits of the classroom gerbil can help him when he reads about hamsters. If he understands the habits of his classroom pet, he will recognize that gerbils not only look a lot like hamsters, but their behavior is similar as well.

The area of processing involves many skills that must work together. Some of the skills needed in order for your child to understand what he reads involve understanding cause and effect, putting ideas in order (sequencing), knowing that the word meaning stays the same even if an *s* or *ed* is added, understanding abstract language, focusing on the materials at hand, and organizing information into the right compartments. The evaluation will let you know if your child has weaknesses in this area.

What a reading evaluation will not tell you is how your child is feeling about herself. No matter how intelligent they are, most children with reading disabilities think they are dumb. Chapter 3, "Self-Esteem," deals with these feelings in depth.

As you can see, the question many parents are often afraid to ask—"Does my child have dyslexia?"—is not so simple to answer. The reading process is extremely complex, and any difficulty your child is having must be looked into with that complexity in mind. You don't want a simple yes or no answer. You can confidently ask what can be done to help your child learn to read or to be a better reader. This question can be answered with a thorough evaluation. You and your child's teachers will have the information you need to design an educational plan to help your child.

What Can You Do at Home

There are many things you can do at home to help improve your child's reading. First and foremost, read to him. Encourage a love of reading. Explore the many worlds that are open to him through reading. Children learn by following parents' examples, and if they see you enjoy reading, they will see it as a pleasurable activity. A child is never too old to be read to. We usually stop doing this when our children read on their own, but many families continue to enjoy reading aloud throughout their lives.

As you read to your child, put your finger under each word as you read it. You will be showing that each word has a visual image and that you read the words in sequence from left to right.

If you find reading difficult, tell your child stories. You will broaden her vocabulary and help her explore areas she could not enter on her own.

Play games that help your child recognize the sounds in words. Our book *Thinking Games to Play with Your Child* has many good examples. Point out sounds that you hear every day and discuss how they are alike or different from other sounds. Do the same thing with what you see. Use the opportunity of a day in the park to explore the differences and similarities between a blue jay and a sparrow, between an oak leaf and a maple leaf. Help your child see how pictures are used to convey ideas on billboards.

Commercial games that require your child to remember and repeat sound patterns provide good practice. You can play a visual concentration game with an ordinary deck of cards or you can make your own deck with letters or words or family pictures. When you go shopping, you can keep your child occupied by having her locate certain letters or shapes in store displays.

There are also things you can do to help your child understand his reading difficulty and minimize his feelings of hopelessness and frustration. Many of the most important minds in our history had reading difficulties. Read biographies of Nelson Rockefeller, Gen. George S. Patton, Thomas Edison, Tom Cruise, Albert Einstein, Cher, and Magic Johnson. They all excelled despite their learning disabilities. Explain the problem to your child openly and honestly. He may not believe you and may think you are only trying to make him feel better, but don't give up.

Encourage his creative side as well. Dancing, singing, or acting can be rewarding outlets.

Allow your child a few "crutches" to help her learn until her reading skills improve. Books on tape can be lots of fun. Read her schoolwork with her if it takes her too long by herself. Let her teacher know that you are doing this so he or she will understand why there is an improvement in the child's work from home. (General Patton had someone read for him at West Point.) Work closely with the school to make sure that your child is learning the other concepts she needs to learn even if she has difficulty reading about them.

Chapter 11

Writing Disabilities

"As soon as you have finished copying your homework assignment, you may line up at the door for recess," the teacher said.

Most of the students in the second grade copied their assignments quickly and were fidgeting at the door waiting for Jamal. They always had to wait for Jamal, and they usually let him know they didn't like it.

Jamal was just as eager to get outside as the other students. In fact, he felt like throwing his paper and his pencil in the wastebasket and forgetting about homework. It took him so long to copy his assignment, he wondered how the others could finish so quickly. Even though he spent more time than the other students copying his assignment, his parents could seldom read what he had written. The entire process was an enormous source of frustration for him.

Though he was one of the more gifted students in the class and read well above grade level, Jamal didn't feel particularly good about himself. His papers were never displayed on the classroom bulletin board, and his artwork never made it to the refrigerator door. He didn't feel good about his written work. He couldn't even zip his own jacket or tie his shoes. He was convinced he was the "dumbest kid in the class."

Jamal's teacher recognized his weaknesses and recommended an evaluation. When students have trouble controlling their small muscles, especially those in the hands, they are said to have fine motor disabilities. Jamal could not make his fingers work in coordination with his thumb. He could not grasp a pencil correctly. He could not use scissors or make his hands cooperate with each other. He hated puzzles and didn't like to play any game that involved small pieces. His disability not only affected his handwriting, but he couldn't do any of the "hands-on" activities offered in his math and science classes. Jamal needed help.

Jamal suffers from a variety of disabilities that affect his writing performance. In addition to his small motor difficulties, Jamal also has problems with sensory integration (getting the information in through his senses in order to be able to use higher level coordination skills).

With reading, math, and receptive language, information is taken into your child's working brain. When he is called on to write, he must be able to organize the information that comes in through the senses, respond appropriately, and get the information out in a way that is understandable and legible.

Our senses tell us what is going on with our body and with the world around us. This information comes in through seeing, hearing, touching, smelling. The information must then go to the brain to be organized in order for us to move, learn, and behave normally. If the flow of information is interrupted or disorganized, it will not be put together in a way that the brain can make sense of and use. For a child with poor sensory integration skills, the nerves and muscles may work fine, but the brain may have difficulty putting all of the information together.

After his evaluation, Jamal worked with an occupational therapist who helped strengthen his muscles and provided sensory integration therapy. Though his writing skills have improved somewhat, Jamal will be a lot happier when his writing assignments can be done on a typewriter or a computer.

When specialists convinced Jamal that he was having trouble with his hands, not with his intellect, his self-esteem improved. Once his learning disability was diagnosed, his teacher began writing Jamal's assignments in his homework book for him. It saved Jamal an enormous amount of frustration, and it made his classmates a lot happier.

The expectation to draw and write begins early in the kindergarten years. By the time they are six years old, children with average fine motor abilities can draw recognizable circles, squares, and crosses, though they may not be perfectly formed. Most can print their first names. Children with difficulties in the area of writing have significant trouble reproducing shapes, including letters and numbers. They may have problems because they do not have the fine motor control necessary to write, or they may have difficulty because their muscles do not "remember" the patterns necessary to form shapes, letters, or numbers. Their difficulty can also result from the inability to use their eyes and hands together.

Because most classroom activity involves fine motor skills—writing, painting, drawing, manipulating objects—children with problems in this area are often frustrated. Sometimes, like Jamal, they feel like failures even though they may be the brightest students in the class. Others might resist any activities that require writing and miss out on important practice to reinforce skills, to create imaginative stories, or to solve math problems.

Children's muscle abilities develop at different rates. Some children are just not ready to write at kindergarten age. They may not have had much practice holding a pencil or crayon and need to strengthen the muscles in the hand and learn the proper way to grasp a pencil. Not all children with delays in this area have learning disabilities. Some simply need a little more time for their muscles to develop, and some need extra practice in school and at home. Others have problems that interfere with their school progress. For these students, intervention is essential.

Michael's first grade teacher was concerned because he did not hold his pencil correctly. Michael wrote his sentences from the right side of the page to the left. A typical sentence might look like this: *klaw a rof tnew god ehT* (The dog went for a walk). The specialist suggested the teacher try activities to strengthen Michael's hand muscles, demonstrate the correct pencil grasp for him, and mark the left side of the page where Michael should begin his sentences. It worked. Michael's written work improved dramatically.

For students with disabilities in this area, written work is usually uneven, poorly spaced, and difficult to read. These children are painfully slow at writing. Often they look awkward while trying to write. Their hands are contorted, their posture is strange, and they look stressed. They usually avoid activities like drawing, coloring, copying, and cutting. They might also have difficulty with the zippers, snaps, buttons, and laces on their clothes.

Children might have the necessary muscle development to write well, but their visual perception causes handwriting difficulties. These children have problems "seeing" likenesses and differences in similar objects. A *d* must be written differently from a *b*. The word *saw* must be written differently from the word *was*. A *9* must be written differently from a *6*. Though this is not a disability in the area of writing, it certainly affects a child's ability to write.

Memory problems can also be a factor in poorly written work. As with reading and math, your child must remember what she has seen long enough to use it. When she is copying from the board, she must look up at the letter or word and then look at her paper to do the copying. She must remember the letter or word, remember the way it is formed, and copy that form on her paper. Some children can't remember what they have seen long enough to get it down. For some, the muscles just don't "remember" the proper sequence to correctly develop shapes.

For some children, forming letters and numbers does not become automatic, and they must think about how to do it each time. Imagine how it would be for you if you had to think about how to pick up your fork, how to use it to pick up food, and how to get it to your mouth each time you eat. Your eating would be very slow and awkward. You surely would find mealtime a stressful experience. That is exactly what happens each time these children try to write.

Spatial organization is necessary for your child to be able to understand how objects relate to each other on paper. This is a necessary skill for writing (placing the letters and words on a page) and in lining up math problems.

A child without these difficulties might write: *The dog went for a walk.* A child with spatial organization problems might write the same sentence this way: *Thedogw entf orawalk.*

Many children with this disability find it easier to write in cursive script than to print. Most find it much easier to write on lined paper than unlined.

Spatial problems can create difficulties when completing a row of math problems. Those without spatial difficulties might write their problems as follows:

$$\begin{array}{r} 235.00 \\ +124.33 \\ \hline 359.33 \end{array} \qquad \begin{array}{r} 123.33 \\ +578.66 \\ \hline 701.99 \end{array}$$

A child with spatial problems, in contrast, might write his first problem in an inappropriate space on the page and then record his numbers in the wrong spaces. If he records the information incorrectly, he cannot come up with the correct answer.

$$\begin{array}{r} 235 \\ +321 \\ \hline 2671 \end{array}$$

Instead of recording his second problem to the right of the first, he might put it somewhere else on the page instead.

$$\begin{array}{l} 424 \\ \underline{+\ 321} \\ 42721 \end{array}$$

These children do not have trouble with the computation. They simply do not have the spatial organization skills to place their numbers in the appropriate columns. They do not "see" or use spaces in the appropriate way. Graph paper helps these students line up their numbers correctly.

Most of these writing abilities occur naturally. If your child is having difficulty writing, he can be helped. A thorough evaluation by an occupational therapist can pinpoint areas of difficulty in order to develop an appropriate remediation plan. School specialists may recommend that a child dictate his written work. If he is not required to do the actual writing, his frustration level is reduced and his opportunities for creativity are expanded. The classroom teacher may allow additional time for written assignments and tests. The specialist may suggest that your child develop keyboard skills in order to type his assignments on a typewriter or word processor.

Many parents worry when specialists suggest compensating for poor written work by typing or having someone else record the child's creative projects. They believe these activities will prevent their child from ever developing improved written skills. Usually specialists recommend this type of compensation during creative projects where a child's poor handwriting skills can inhibit the creative thought process. There is no need to hold your child back during these critical thinking sessions. In addition to using these compensation techniques, most specialists suggest that children continue to develop their handwriting skills during specific sessions designed to strengthen fine motor skills, memory skills, and/or spatial skills.

However, some children's disabilities are so severe they will never write with the clarity or speed necessary to produce written materials. For these children, typing and word processing are life skills they will rely on whenever they need to communicate in writing.

In addition to those activities planned during school time, there are many activities that can be done at home to help strengthen writing skills.

What You Can Do at Home

To help your child improve his writing skills, encourage him to work to strengthen his large and small muscles. Activities that emphasize overall body strength and sensory awareness, like walking, running, skipping, hopping, jumping, stretching, bending, dancing, crawling, and swimming, can improve your child's overall motor coordination. Hopscotch is a good game to use for many of these movements. Jump rope and Simon Says are also good.

To develop hand strength, involve your child in play activities that use Play-Doh or Silly Putty. Activities that can strengthen hand muscles include opening clothespins, punching holes in paper with a hand-held hole punch, squeezing the trigger on a water pistol, stringing pop beads, squeezing bulb-shaped bicycle horns, operating wind-up toys and using tweezers to move pieces of rice into patterns.

Eye-hand coordination can be developed by stringing beads or buttons, or by working with puzzles, peg boards, Legos, stickers, and building blocks. Etch-A-Sketch is a commercial toy drawing screen that requires fine motor skills. Rediscover the fun in a game of marbles or pick-up sticks.

When you play games with your child, be sure to point out the visual characteristics of the activity. For example, talk about the shape, color, and size of the puzzle and game pieces. When reading to your child, remark about the objects in the pictures and talk about how those objects relate to the story you are reading. Encourage her to play games that require matching and sorting, such as concentration played with a deck of cards.

Games like horseshoes, ring toss, and bean bags require your child to use his eyes and hands together. T ball, baseball, bowling, and Ping-Pong are also good games to develop coordination.

A very popular picture book with today's children is *Where's Waldo?* Most children find it challenging and fun to search for the Waldo character in a sea of other characters. Children's magazines often have puzzles with hidden objects or messages. Some children love to find the cat in the pond or the dog perched in the tree.

Children who have weaknesses in the areas addressed in these activities may be reluctant to play. Keep trying. Remember to praise your child for the creative thoughts he has recorded on paper rather than criticizing the way he recorded his thoughts. For all children, critical and creative thinking skills are the most important.

Chapter 12

Math Disabilities

Josh, an eighth grade student, had a great relationship with his parents. He was an active child and a member of his middle school soccer team. The house was always full of his friends. He and his parents could talk about almost anything—anything except math. When Josh had to do his math homework, he became a different person.

"He took on a completely different personality," his mother confided. "I wondered what happened to my real son."

When Josh had to do math, he became sullen and noncommunicative. He wasted time, crumbled his papers, and swore. He just didn't want to do it. Merely looking at a page of numbers made him angry. The numbers made no sense; the concepts made no sense.

Josh had received D's in math ever since the second grade. No one seemed too concerned because his other grades were usually A's or B's.

"He just doesn't have a head for numbers...Just like his mother," people laughed.

No one suspected that Josh had a learning disability in the area of math. He never received special help until eighth grade.

When children have difficulties with reading and language, their parents are usually the first to notice. But when they have trouble with math, parents are among the last to recognize the problem. Many adults find math troublesome and so they stay away from it. If their children have math difficulties, they don't consider it a learning disability but simply an absence of talent in the area of mathematics.

Of the parents we talked with, fathers seemed more concerned about math problems than mothers did. Many of the mothers had difficulty with math themselves. When their children had trouble with math, they didn't think it was anything unusual, and it was a relatively acceptable disability. Expectations in this area were not as high. If a child cannot read, the reasoning goes, he must have a learning disability. If the child can't do math, it's because he just isn't good at it.

Difficulties with math don't surface as often in school as other learning disabilities and often are not addressed as aggressively. Difficulties with reading and language spill over into almost every phase of a child's educational life. Not so with math. For some reason, we expect all children to learn to read and write. We don't expect all of them to be good at math. In fact, remedial classes and special education classes are designed to work more with reading problems than with math problems. However, if your child, like Josh, is reduced to tears struggling over his math homework or can't come home with the correct change after shopping, you know he has a problem. And you worry.

You are correct in your concern. Research has documented "dyscalculia" as an inability to work with figures. Less extreme forms of math disabilities can also affect your child's progress in math and science classes in school and can have a profound effect on self-esteem.

A difficulty in math can be a definite handicap in school and in the job market, and it can also be a signal that your child has other learning problems. Terry, a second grader, can read books at the second grade level and do math computation at a second grade level. However, she has no idea of the value of money or time and she really doesn't know what numbers mean. She has learned to count by memory, but she can't name the number that comes before or after a particular number. When her mother tells her to get ready because they will be going out in five minutes, Terry isn't sure whether that is a short time or a long time. This type of learning disability can affect reading comprehension as well.

Mathematics is more than just working with numbers. Schools are becoming more aware of the importance of developing mathematical thinking skills to help foster abilities in problem-solving. A good foundation in math encourages logical thinking and risk-taking. These are important skills for any child.

Mathematics is a language system, and an evaluation of a disability in math must be conducted with this in mind. When your child learns to read, he learns a set of abstract symbols that he must put together to make words and sentences. The same happens in math. Numbers are abstract symbols that are put together to make number sentences. Your child must understand these symbols and the basic concepts of how they go together in order to solve the problems presented in these sentences.

Your child must understand the language of math. This involves recognizing the symbols used in the math problem, working with the symbols, and arriving at a solution to the problem. The symbols used for math include numbers, number combinations, shapes, and signs. The symbols are the concrete aspects of math. They do not change, and the quantities they represent can be demonstrated with actual objects. Your child must remember the symbol (memory) and remember it in the order in which he sees it (sequential memory). He has to understand what the symbol represents, and he must realize that the symbol can be used in a variety of ways. He must understand numbers, know which numbers come before and after others, and be able to compare, estimate, and compute.

Many abilities must come together in order for your child to recognize these symbols. Your child needs to know the difference between the numbers 1 and 2, and she must also be able to tell the difference between 12 and 21. She needs to recognize that 1, 2, 12, and 21 contain the same symbols but the symbols mean different things.

Some children have reversal problems with number symbols. They might not be able to see the difference between 9 and 6. Though many young children have problems with reversals, by second grade typical children are no longer confused.

Other children have problems with discrimination. They might not see the difference between a square and a rectangle. Some have problems with sequencing. Imagine the frustration of a third grader who was able to work a problem correctly but consistently wrote the answer incorrectly. Instead of 324, he wrote 423.

Difficulties with math may also be the result of a visual perception problem. Your child may have trouble lining up problems on the paper and may become confused when it is time to work with the numbers he has written. He will not be able to add a vertical sequence of numbers if they are not written in an even row. This difficulty with spatial relations can have an impact on math performance.

Assuming your child has no difficulties with reversals, discrimination, or perception, she could still have problems remembering all possible addition, subtraction, and multiplication combinations needed to solve problems.

In order to work with math symbols, once she knows them, your child must have a working understanding of other aspects of the language of math. She must understand the word clues in a math sentence. For example, when a word problem asks, "How much is left?" she must know to subtract. If the problem asks, "How many all together?," she must know to add or multiply.

She must also understand the concepts of time and space. What do *before, after, many,* or *few,* actually mean? She must be able to estimate and to make numerical predictions. She must see the connections and relationships between the numbers and the words of a problem and be able to translate them into mathematical computations. She must be able to organize the information in a way that makes sense. This might involve the use of measurement techniques, geometric figures, graphs, and charts.

Other children have trouble paying attention to details. If the first half of their homework assignment is made up of addition problems, they may continue to add through the second half of the assignment even though the later problems call for subtraction.

Because so much of the math computation children perform in school is done in a group setting, children with problems in math are often put on the spot. Each student must compute the problem on the board, or must give the answer aloud. There is usually only one right answer. If he makes a mistake, everyone knows it. The minute he writes the answer to a math problem on the blackboard or says it aloud in class, it is too late to take it back. The child who is unsure of his math ability is often afraid to take this risk. This type of pressure can cause math phobia.

Josh's fear of math affected his behavior. Every time he needed to open his math book and begin work, he would do something to get himself into trouble. He knew if he was sent out of the room, he wouldn't have to do his math assignment. He was so sure that he would get the problem wrong, he would rather risk punishment for misbehaving than endure his failure in front of his peers.

Math can and should be fun for you and your child. If your child has a learning disability in the area of math, however, math isn't fun. A thorough evaluation can provide insight into the appropriate teaching method to use to help your child learn all that he is capable of learning.

What You Can Do at Home

Parents of children with math disabilities often assume they are responsible for the difficulties. When a teacher tells them their child has difficulty remembering his math facts, they may assume they have not spent enough time drilling the child at home. Many said they felt guilty. They shouldn't. Children with learning disabilities in math may not respond to traditional math drills. They may need other strategies to help them learn.

There are many things you can do at home to help your child become more comfortable with math. Don't shy away from these activities. If you are reluctant to play math games, your child will learn from your example that math is not fun. In fact, math can be a lot of fun if you don't have to write anything down or be tested. The book *Thinking Games to Play with Your Child* has many games you can play at home, in the car, or away from home to encourage mathematical thinking.

If you don't like math or math games, try to keep your dislike to yourself. Your negative comments can validate your child's negative feelings. "I always hated math too" does little to increase a child's interest in numbers.

Make a game of the chores around the house and encourage counting at the same time. When folding laundry, see who can find the most socks. When setting the table, see who can put down the most complete set of utensils first. Think aloud in questions and use the language of math. For example, "If Aunt Joan and Uncle Stephen are coming for dinner, how many more plates will I have to put on the table?" If you use this mathematical language at home, children will be more comfortable and familiar with it when they hear it at school.

It is not necessary for your child to come up with the answer each time you pose a mathematical question. You just want to encourage him to think "math" and realize that it is not a foreign language. Point out quantity and time concepts whenever possible.

For example, "We will be taking this package to your uncle in five minutes. That's not much time, so hurry and get ready."

Notice that you have *more* cereal in your bowl than he does, or that he must brush his teeth *BEFORE* going to bed rather than *AFTER.*

Count as you go up and down steps and occasionally jump over a step and skip that number in your counting. Explain money to your child and show that sometimes you don't have enough to pay for an item. When you get change, explain that you gave the cashier more money than necessary. Encourage your child to pay for things and give her practice using money.

Use a chalkboard at home for writing math messages. Colored chalk is more fun than plain white. Keep a supply of graph paper handy and use it for drawing pictures, maps, or anything else you can think of.

Make practice fun by playing a concentration-type game to review math facts. Put the problems on a series of cards. Place the answers on other cards. When your child turns over the 5 + 3 card, he will need to remember where the 8 card is to make his match.

Sometimes it is necessary to put objects on the cards along with the numbers. Place the correct number of circles above each number to help them understand exactly what the numbers represent.

○○○○○		○○○		○○○○ ○○○○
5	+	3	=	8

Let your child use a calculator to check her answers. It is quick and fun. Some children will always need to rely on calculators to perform basic mathematical operations.

The best thing you can do for children with disabilities in math is to create an environment where math just happens. Math should be a natural part of your daily activities, not a process to be completed when it is time to take a test. Help your child to relax and to see that playing with numbers can be fun.

Chapter 13

Testing and Evaluations

When Esther received a letter from her son's school, she was confused and worried. It was a form letter sent to the parent of every child in the kindergarten class. According to the letter, a routine screening by the special education department showed that Lee had some areas of weakness, and the special education team recommended he have an evaluation.

Esther never suspected there was anything wrong with Lee's learning. He had gone to preschool for two years prior to kindergarten, and there had never been any word from his preschool teachers about any problems. She had done everything she knew she was supposed to do. She or her husband read to Lee every night, and they made sure that they spent a lot of time in children's museums and libraries. She involved him in play groups as well as preschool, and he got along fine with other children.

When she stopped to consider the letter, she realized only one thing had ever concerned her about his learning. Even though she provided him with paper, crayons, markers, and pencils, Lee did not enjoy drawing or writing. She could not persuade him to put anything on paper. He preferred to play outside, and she felt the physical activity was more important to him. It never occurred to her that his reluctance to write or draw might affect his academic performance. Now, the special educators were saying they suspected her son had a problem. She found that troubling.

Most parents react the same way. The first phases of an evaluation process are often the most stressful for parents. As they learn more about the process, the evaluators, and the tests, they usually begin to feel more comfortable. In fact, once they have more information about the evaluation process, most parents look forward to finding information that will help their child learn better. Everyone benefits from having the information provided, and the child begins to have a more successful school experience.

One of the reasons parents find the evaluation process upsetting is that adults often associate evaluations with test-taking and the related anxiety. For the most part, however, children enjoy being tested. It is a time when they receive individual attention and praise from an adult. Children might even receive stickers or rewards for working hard. What could be better than that?

Most parents have questions when school officials recommend their child have an evaluation. What is an evaluation anyway? What are the evaluators looking for? What will they see in my son or daughter that I don't know? What will they find out about me? Will they judge me as a parent? What did I do wrong? What should I have done?

When you agree to have your child evaluated, you will want answers to those questions and you will want to know how the evaluation process works. The purpose of any evaluation is to discover your child's strengths and weaknesses and to understand how he learns and where he has difficulty. This information is used to help you and the school provide the best possible learning environment for your child.

There are a variety of methods of evaluation. Those your child needs are determined by his age and the type of problem he appears to have. In most cases, he will be evaluated in more than one area. This will ensure that no single evaluation is used to make decisions about your child. In Lee's case, his reluctance to write might indicate that the evaluation should center on the area of his fine motor skills. However, if the team only looked at his fine motor skills, they might overlook other areas that might be contributing to his difficulties. Visual memory problems or attention problems could also be factors.

Before any child is tested, parents are notified of possible weaknesses in the child's skills. A meeting is usually scheduled with the parents and a representative from the special education department. At this meeting, the specialist discusses the teacher's concerns regarding the child's educational progress. The specialist explains which tests are being recommended, who will give the tests, where the tests will be given, and how long the process will take. The special educator also provides parents with a copy of their rights. The specialist will ask for written permission to perform any recommended tests, and no tests will be administered without parental permission.

Specific tests are designed to determine if a child has a specific learning disability. Specialists usually recommend beginning the evaluation process with a general academic overview to determine if any areas of weakness are affecting a child's academic performance. This type of educational evaluation can be given to all children, even those who have not yet had formal education. The test is usually administered by a specialist in learning disabilities.

The first part of this type of an educational evaluation looks at what your child can do. If she is school age, it will test her ability in reading, spelling, math, and any other relevant subjects. At younger ages it looks at her ability to use numbers and words and to see likenesses and differences in them. This test also looks at how she processes information through hearing and seeing. The tester will be looking for any area where the educational process breaks down.

The tester will be able to determine if your child learns better through hearing or seeing or a combination of both. A child who is a strong visual learner, and who is weak at picking up information through hearing, might need to be taught to read with an emphasis on what she sees (sight approach) rather than what she hears (phonics approach). This information can be helpful at home. It might indicate that instructions and information you give at home might best be presented with pictures and written instructions rather than through verbal commands.

This overall evaluation will also tell you where your child's skills are in relation to others his age and will let you and his teachers know where to begin in teaching him. If his number skills are at a three-year-old level, you do not want to frustrate him by expecting him to combine numbers at a six-year-old-level. The work begins where he is and continues from there.

Many parents also choose to have their child take a psychological test at this time. These tests are administered by a certified psychologist and usually consist of two parts. The first part is an individual intelligence test. This provides information on a child's intellectual potential or IQ. The results of this type of test can vary depending on how the child feels at the time of testing.

The other part of a psychological evaluation is an assessment of emotions. It looks for anything that might be bothering the child to the extent that it could interfere with his learning. For this test, children are asked to look at a series of pictures and create a story about them. The pictures are fairly standard and show a variety of normal situations. The psychologist looks for themes that emerge in relation to more than one picture story. That gives an indication of what is on the child's mind that could be interfering with learning.

An interview with parents is an important part of a psychological evaluation. Without a parent's involvement, the themes that emerge may be misleading. Five-year-old Jessica told the psychologist stories about abandonment and loneliness. When the psychologist talked to Jessica's mother, she learned that Jessica's father was in the Merchant Marines and had left that morning for his usual stint. It was perfectly normal for Jessica to have temporary feelings of loneliness at his departure. Feelings of anger or disappointment may also affect a child's performance on any test, and it is important to keep this in mind when evaluating the test results.

Another aspect of the emotional section of the evaluation might be having a child draw a self-portrait or a picture of the family.

Some parents say they feel uncomfortable or anxious about the emotional aspect of the tests. It is rare, however, for anything to show up here that the parents do not already sense. If there is a problem, most parents want to deal with it. In order to help a child learn, it is important to get as much information as possible to put together a total picture. Parents may request a meeting with the psychologist before testing to provide any information about their child they feel may affect the test.

A developmental history, or social assessment, may also be recommended. The specialist who does the assessment interviews the parents. The evaluation might include questions about when the child began to walk and talk and how she gets along with family and friends. (It is a good idea to keep a diary that lists when the child did certain things for the first time. That way you can be as accurate as possible.)

Other questions in this development history might ask about pregnancy and family history. These questions are not meant to cast blame or guilt. They help to focus attention and remediation where it can be most effective. If there are medical or family reasons for a child's disability, even the best remediation strategies won't work until those issues are taken into consideration. The answers to these questions are additional puzzle pieces that fit together to get a total picture of the child.

Another group of tests addresses specific areas of learning. If professionals suggest your child have one of these tests, it is important for you to know what they will be looking for. A speech and language evaluation is given by a certified speech and language pathologist or therapist. This test examines your child's ability to understand language and his ability to express himself. It also looks at how well he speaks based on the sounds that he should be able to pronounce at his age. If your child has difficulty understanding spoken or written language, it will interfere with his performance on all other tests that expect him to understand and follow oral or written directions.

An occupational therapy evaluation examines fine motor skills, visual-motor integration, and sensory integration. This type of test is not routinely given unless there are extreme concerns about the way a child's nerves and muscles work together or the way she organizes information. Psychological and educational assessments look at fine motor areas, too, and can usually give a good indication of whether there is a need for a specialized evaluation by an occupational therapist.

Gross motor skills, muscle tone, and balance are evaluated by a physical therapist. If there are concerns in this area, the determination for an evaluation is usually made by the child's physician, who is the best person to determine if the child's physical development might create a problem in school.

Once parents have decided to have their child evaluated, the next question they ask is where the evaluation should take place. If your child is younger than three years old and you are concerned, by law your child is entitled to testing. Parents can contact the Early Intervention Office in their area to see what type of services and testing they provide. The state department of public health or your local school system should be able to provide you with their number. The Early Intervention Office should be able to arrange testing for your child or refer you to the appropriate agency.

If your child is at least three years old, he can be evaluated through your local school system. There are many advantages to having testing done there. The school atmosphere provides a more normal environment for your child. If he is already in school, the evaluation can take place during the school day without a major interruption of his routine. If he is not yet in school, he will at least see other children in the school and see toys and books similar to those at home. A school evaluation is usually not as threatening as a hospital evaluation or a test taken at an evaluation center. Furthermore, if a learning problem is discovered, the school will develop a plan for helping your child learn. If your local school system has done the testing, it will be easier for them to develop the plan. When you work with the school system, you initiate a long, close relationship with your child's teachers that begins with trust and a common outlook about your child.

Sometimes parents have specific doubts or concerns about their particular school system and prefer to have an independent evaluation. Unfortunately, this sometimes creates an uncomfortable relationship between the parents and the schools. Sometimes a school system will not accept the results of an outside evaluation without doing testing on its own. This will mean that your child has to be tested twice. This can increase anxiety in your child. Why not start with your school system? If you disagree with the evaluation of the school, you can always go to a hospital or evaluation center for a second opinion.

If you choose to have an independent evaluation, there are many places that provide this service. The list of advocacy groups in Appendices B and C of this book will help you locate an agency that will offer what you want. Be sure you ask questions about the agency you are considering to ensure that you will get the information you want. Find out the qualifications of the members of their evaluation team, which tests will be given, and how the results will be reported. You need to feel comfortable with the facility in order to help your child relax. It is a good idea to let your child's school know that the child is having the evaluation. Their opinion will be important in establishing the total picture of your child.

Whether your child is tested at school, a hospital, or an evaluation center, your role is important in preparing him for the evaluation. If he feels that you are concerned about the results, he will also be concerned. You need to tell your child why he is being evaluated. Tell him you want some information to determine how he learns best. He probably knows that he is having some difficulty, and this explanation will make sense to him.

If your school system has recommended an evaluation, or if you suspect your child may have some learning difficulties, begin the process as soon as possible. Once you have all the information you need to feel comfortable with the process, there is no reason to wait.

Some of the tests that may be recommended for your child are described here to help you get started. If your school system administers different tests, you can ask for similar explanations of the areas tested and the meaning of the results.

Tests of Educational and Specific Learning Disabilities

The ANSER System (Aggregate Neurobehavioral Student Health and Educational Review)

Ages: 3 years to 12+

This questionnaire, developed under the direction of Melvin D. Levine, M.D., F.A.A.P., is used by parents and schools to provide guidelines for looking at educational, developmental, behavioral, and health issues. The answers to the questions provide a profile of your child from more than one source. This questionnaire is often used to help determine a diagnosis of ADHD or ADD. Different forms are used depending upon the child's age. The results are usually interpreted by the child's physician.

The Brigance Comprehensive Inventory of Basic Skills

Grades: Preschool through grade 9

This inventory looks at what your child knows in 22 different skill areas. It helps to identify areas where your child needs additional work and can be used in developing specific objectives for your child's educational plan.

Bruininks-Oseretsky Test of Motor Proficiency

Ages: 4½ years to 14½

This is a test of fine and gross motor abilities. It is usually administered by an occupational therapist and is helpful in developing a motor training program if one is needed.

Detroit Tests of Learning Aptitude

Ages: 3 years through 9, or 6 years through 18 (depending upon the version used)

This test measures intelligence, language, attention, and motor abilities and is useful in diagnosing specific learning disabilities in those areas. It assesses how your child processes information, how her attention level affects her performance, and how her written response enhances or inhibits her ability to perform. There are two forms of this test—an abbreviated version for younger children and a longer form for older children.

Developmental Test of Visual-Motor Coordination (sometimes called the Beery Test)

Ages: 4 years through 13

This test measures your child's eye-hand coordination skills by asking him to copy geometric figures. The figures are arranged in order of increasing difficulty; each figure is scored pass/fail. The results are interpreted by the evaluator and are reported in age equivalents.

Gesell Institute of Human Development Preschool Test

Ages: 2½ years through 6

This test is designed to evaluate your child's developmental level in the area of gross motor skills, fine motor skills, language skills, and personal-social skills. It was originally intended to be used to determine if a child was ready for kindergarten, but it can also be used to determine your child's ability level in the above areas and help plan remediation in those areas, if necessary.

Gray Oral Reading Tests—Revised

Ages: 6 years through 17

These tests measure growth in oral reading and provide diagnostic information about oral reading difficulties. Rate and comprehension are assessed.

Kaufman Test of Educational Achievement (KTEA)

Ages: 6 years through 18

This is an individual achievement test that measures what your child knows in the areas of reading, math, and spelling. The test provides an in-depth analysis of achievement that can be used in program planning and in writing individual educational plans (IEPs).

Key Math, Revised—A Diagnostic Inventory of Essential Mathematics

Grades: Kindergarten through grade 9

This is a test of important mathematical concepts generally covered in kindergarten through grade 9 curricula. It is designed to show specific strengths and weaknesses in math and to help plan a remediation program if necessary. The areas assessed are basic concepts (time, money, measurement, geometry, sequencing, estimating), operations (addition, subtraction, multiplication, division), and application (problem-solving).

Pre-Reading Screening Procedures to Identify First Grade Academic Needs—Revised

Grades: Kindergarten through beginning grade 1

This is a test for children who have not yet been introduced to reading. It assesses skills needed in order to learn to read. It can identify strengths and weaknesses in learning styles.

Slingerland Screening Tests for Identifying Children with Specific Language Disabilities

Grades: 1 through 6

This test is designed to give an indication of whether your child has a specific language disability that will interfere with reading, writing, spelling, or speaking. The specific areas evaluated are visual-motor coordination, visual memory, visual discrimination, auditory-visual discrimination, and auditory memory-to-motor ability. The different sections or subtests are designed to be administered in an atmosphere resembling an actual classroom as opposed to a one-on-one testing situation.

Test of Visual-Perceptual Skills (Non-Motor) (sometimes called The Gardner Test)

Ages: 4 years through 12

This test evaluates your child's ability to understand and interpret what he sees. By allowing him to point to the answer rather than write it, motor ability or disability is not a factor and does not interfere in the interpretation of the results. Therefore, the skills being assessed are mainly visual. The specific skills measured include discrimination, memory, spatial relationships, form constancy, sequential memory, figure-ground, and closure.

Test of Written Language (TOWL)

Ages: 7 years through 17

This test uses an essay format as well as an objective answer format to get an understanding of how your child organizes information in order to write it down. The areas measured include vocabulary, thematic maturity, handwriting, spelling, word usage, and grammar.

Wide Range Achievement Test—R (WRAT-R)

Ages: 5 years through adult

This is a relatively quick test of reading, spelling, and math. It provides a grade score but does not provide diagnostic or remedial information. The reading section measures the ability to recognize letters and words. It does not measure comprehension. This test is usually given when time is a factor or to indicate whether more extensive testing is needed.

Woodcock-Johnson Psychoeducational Battery, Revised

Grades: Preschool through adult

This battery is divided into three sections. The first section measures your child's cognitive (intellectual) abilities. These include long- and short-term memory, processing speed of visual and auditory information, understanding of information, and the ability to shift from one task to another. It also gives a measure of your child's aptitude in the academic skills. The achievement section measures reading, math, written language, and knowledge. A third section measures interest. The results show the difference between what your child is capable of learning and what he is actually learning. Many systems use this difference (or discrepancy) to determine whether a child is eligible for special education services. The scores compare your child to other children of her age and in her grade. They also compare her achievement to her ability.

Psychological Tests

Bender Visual Motor Gestalt Test

Ages: 5 years through 11

This is a widely used psychological and visual-motor test. It provides information on eye-hand coordination, including motor planning and organization, and it can indicate the presence of emotional problems such as impulsivity and anxiety. The results should be interpreted as part of an overall battery of tests.

Draw a Person

Ages: 3 years to 10

The results of this test can be interpreted in a variety of ways. It is a good screening measure of nonverbal intelligence for children. The child is asked to draw a human figure. He receives points for each of the body parts drawn. The complexity of the drawing gives an indication of the child's intellectual maturity. Because it is a picture of a person, your child's interpretation of the person can give some indication of his self-concept. The results should be interpreted as part of an overall battery of tests.

Slosson Intelligence Test—Revised (SIT-R)

Ages: 4 years to adult

This intelligence test can be administered by an educational specialist as part of an educational evaluation. It is a quick measure of intelligence and relies heavily on language. It tests general knowledge, comprehension, arithmetic, similarities and differences, vocabulary, and auditory memory.

Stanford Binet Intelligence Scale

Ages: 2 years through adult

This is an individual general intelligence test that must be given by someone trained in its administration. The results can be interpreted in several ways including verbal comprehension, nonverbal reasoning/visualization, and memory.

Wechsler Intelligence Scale for Children, Revised (WISC-R)

Ages: 6 years through 17

This test provides a good estimate of your child's level of intelligence. It can only be given by someone trained in its administration. It is divided into two parts: verbal and performance. There is a verbal score, a performance score, and a total score. The individual subtests in each part can also be analyzed to provide information about specific strengths and weaknesses as well as attention factors. A different scale is used for preschool children (Wechsler Preschool and Primary Scale of Intelligence—WPPSI).

Speech and Language Tests

Bracken Basic Concept Scale (BBCS)

Ages: 2½ years to 8

This test measures the child's knowledge of general language concepts taught during the first years of school. The areas tested include colors, letters, numbers, comparisons, shapes, direction, social/emotional, size, texture, quantity, and time.

Expressive One-Word Picture Vocabulary Test (EOWPVT)

Ages: 2 years to 12

This test measures your child's ability to express language verbally. He is required to associate pictures with words. It reveals how your child processes language and understands abstract and concrete language, how well he can generalize language concepts, and how well he understands descriptive language.

Goldman-Fristoe Test of Articulation

Ages: 2 years to 16

This test looks at both spontaneous speech and imitative speech to provide a picture of your child's articulation ability in all situations. It measures how she says individual sounds in words and lets you know whether an error occurs at all times, or only at the beginning, middle, or end of words. This type of information is useful in developing strategies for remediation.

Peabody Picture Vocabulary Test—Revised (PPVT)

Ages: 2½ years through adult

This is a test of receptive language vocabulary and verbal ability. Your child is shown four pictures and is asked to point to the one that represents a given word or concept. It does not require reading, writing, or speaking.

Receptive One-Word Picture Vocabulary Test (ROWPVT)

Ages: 2 years through 11

This test measures your child's ability to match an object or concept with its name. It assesses the level of receptive vocabulary development and can be looked at along with the EOWPVT to show the differences, if any, between the child's receptive and expressive vocabulary.

Test of Auditory Comprehension of Language (TACL)

Ages: 3 years through 9

This is a test of receptive language. It is divided into the following categories: word classes and relations, grammar, and elaborated sentences. Your child must point to the picture that shows the concept presented.

Test of Auditory-Perceptual Skills (TAPS)

Ages: 4 years to 12

This test looks at all areas of auditory processing including discrimination, sequential memory, word memory, sentence memory, and interpretation of directions.

Test of Language Development (TOLD)

Ages: 4 years through 12

This test measures how well your child understands and uses spoken language. It looks at how he understands grammar, the concept of a word and a sentence, and his ability to say words and to distinguish between similar sounding words. Abstract language, vocabulary, sentence combining and construction, and word relationships are also explored.

Chapter 14

Finding the Right College

The headmaster stood at the podium. The graduates were seated in front of him and proud parents filled the rows behind. The headmaster was ready to present the school's most prestigious award honoring the school's all-around student.

"Not many students in our memory exhibit these qualities quite so clearly as this year's recipient. As one who has sometimes struggled to attain academic confirmation, he has shown us how hard work, persistence, and true connection with his faculty can result in the realization of his goals. Being a quiet and introspective person, most of how we got to know this student has been through his work as the student coordinator of the Work Program. Through his diligence in this time-consuming task, he has maintained a fair, objective, well-organized, and effective system.

"Kind, selfless, unflappable, and industrious, this gentle giant has improved all our lives by his membership in the school community. It is with great pleasure that we present this 1992 Headmaster's Award to Paul Michael Davis."

Paul's mother beamed. It hadn't been easy, but Paul had just received his high school's highest award.

When Paul started preschool, it was obvious he had serious learning disabilities. In elementary school, he had trouble learning to read, he had trouble speaking, he had trouble interacting with his classmates. His parents, like many parents of children with learning disabilities, wondered if he would ever succeed in school. They worried he would never be able to attend college.

Paul still has serious learning disabilities, but he has learned to compensate. Paul not only succeeded in high school and won his school's most prestigious prize—he begins college this fall.

Paul's family was typical in their worries. When I speak to parents and confirm their suspicions that their child has a learning disability, they often ask me if I think their child will be able to go to college. Many parents regard a college education as essential for their child's success. I tell them that students with average or above intelligence and with the potential to succeed can certainly go to college.

Students with mild learning disabilities have a good chance of succeeding in a college without special services. Those with moderate to severe learning disabilities might be best served at a college that specializes in teaching students with learning disabilities or at a school that provides special support services for LD students. Your child might be able to get into a college without being identified as learning disabled, but he may have to struggle with course work that places him at a disadvantage in his classes. Without help, he risks failure.

The admissions director of a small college in Massachusetts bemoaned the fact that a number of students were being admitted based on their high school grade point averages. The students were successful in high school with the support of a special education staff. Their records did not indicate they had received this type of support. Once they arrived at college, they faltered without help.

Some colleges have support programs for students with learning disabilities, but many don't. If a student has required special services through high school, it is likely he will continue to need them in college. School guidance counselors and your child's teachers can help you and your student decide what type of college is best.

At the level of college admissions, a learning disability is not something to hide or to be ashamed of. In fact, when taking the college aptitude tests like the SAT or the ACT, some students with learning disabilities are offered modifications that allow for their disabilities. Some students benefit from having more time to complete the test. Others find it extremely helpful to have someone read the test to them. The procedures for qualifying for this type of testing are complicated, but for many students with learning disabilities they are well worth the effort. Be sure to check with your child's high school guidance office to see if your child qualifies for this type of testing, or contact the following agencies for more information:

ACT Special Testing
ACT Test Administration
P.O. Box 168
Iowa City, IA 52243
(319) 337-1332

or

Scholastic Aptitude Test (SAT)
Admissions Testing Program for Handicapped Students
CN 6603
Princeton, NJ 08541
(215) 750-8147

Education Testing Service (ETS) has special tests in braille, large-type, cassette, and regular type. They also arrange for other accommodations such as a reader, additional time, and rest periods. Contact them at (609) 921-9000.

If your child has the intelligence and the potential to succeed in college in spite of his learning disability, you deserve to be extremely proud and to take credit for your efforts in helping him maintain his self-esteem and love for learning. Never feel you have to give up your dream for your child's education.

"Don't pay attention to other parents. Don't be discouraged when your friend says, 'My son is going to Harvard,'" one parent advised.

"Gregory's biggest obstacle was getting into college. He made it with some difficulty. He is a good average student. That is an achievement, and we are so proud of him," she said.

One parent I spoke to was told by a doctor at a major hospital that his first grade son would never be able to go to college. This father was devastated that he had to shift his expectations and goals for his son at such an early age. He refused to accept the diagnosis. Further testing through the public school revealed a significant language disability. It also showed the boy's intelligence was above average. Currently, the student is progressing well in high school and is planning to attend college.

Because you want your child to succeed, the decision for your child to attend college must not be taken lightly. Even with special programs and services, college might be a struggle. Remember, most students, even those without learning disabilities, experience some difficulty with the workload, the level of independent study, and the social situations in college. Students with learning disabilities must be even better prepared than most.

While in high school students should focus their attention on developing skills that will help them succeed in college. Organizational skills are a must. They should be keeping a weekly schedule of their activities and assignments. They need to learn to organize their notes and their notebooks.

Those who have trouble taking notes might begin working with a tape recorder in class. The student should continue to take notes and then use the recording to reinforce the material while doing homework.

The tape recorder can also be an asset for those who have difficulty writing. It may be easier to record thoughts verbally than on paper. If writing is difficult or impossible, students may have someone transcribe their tapes for them.

Word processors have made life much easier for students with writing disabilities. Most high schools offer computer courses and keyboard skills. If your high school doesn't, seek out programs at local community colleges or universities.

A recent graduate of Syracuse University said the word processor was his crutch when it came to writing. It could do many of the things he had trouble doing. Spelling? No problem. Most word processors come with "spell checkers." Editing? He didn't have to write several versions of his reports. Once he had his outline in the computer, he could edit as he went along.

Even with the wonders of modern technology, it is useful to have someone proofread papers before they are submitted. This is something parents and tutors can help students with. Those who can proofread their own materials should read them out loud.

Students with difficulties in math should be using calculators. They may be required to take introductory-level math classes in any major, and it is best to be prepared.

Those students who have extreme difficulty reading should explore the option of using books on tape. Recording for the Blind (RFB) is a nonprofit organization that lends recorded educational books to people who can't read standard print because of visual, physical, or specific learning disabilities. In order to qualify for this service, the learning disability must be well documented, and that can take time. Those who will be using this service will need to preregister for college classes and order their books before school begins.

Social interactions are sometimes a problem for students with learning disabilities, and social skills are even more important for college students. High school students should seek out learning disabled students who have already completed their first year or two of college. These experienced college students can help guide new students through the social maze.

Most colleges offer orientation programs for new students. Students with learning disabilities can begin to make social contacts in small groups during this introductory program. Many colleges also offer small-group outdoor programs before the start of the academic year. These often present opportunities for learning disabled students to develop their confidence in an environment where they flourish.

One of the most important skills your child will need when he leaves home is the ability to act as his own advocate. Most parents of children with learning disabilities have spent years advocating for their child. High school is the time to let your child begin doing some of that work for himself. Let him make his own appointments with his guidance counselor. Have him begin to verbalize his special learning needs. Have him tell you what he will need in terms of services from college and help prepare him to ask questions when you visit colleges.

Let him make his own decisions about what he will need when he goes off to school. Now is the time to learn how to manage a checking account. With all he will need to learn during his first months at college, he can be one step ahead of many students if he has learned to manage his finances. If he has never been to a laundromat, make sure he knows how to use a coin-operated washer and dryer.

"Once he gets to school, make four copies of his room key...and give him an attentive voice on the other end of the phone," suggested one parent.

Most important, help guide him through the college search, but let him make the final decision about where he will go to school.

When students with learning disabilities begin their college search, they should meet with their teachers and guidance counselors to help evaluate the areas in which they will need help in college. The counselor can also advise which support services are the most important for your child.

One student at a small New England college visited a resource center whenever she needed to submit a paper for class. A tutor at the center helped her to organize her materials and her thoughts and to get her ideas on paper. In addition, spelling was not counted on her tests. Those were the only services she needed even though this particular college had an extensive program for learning disabled students.

Another student told us his professor read his exam questions out loud for him.

Often the school counselor will know which schools in your area have programs that would be appropriate for your child. Counselors also help guide students through the admissions process. Once students begin examining college programs, they will want to be sure the college offers services to assist in their specific area of disability.

Once Paul and his mother found a college they thought offered the types of services, the program, and the environment that was right for him, they asked his special education teacher to call the school. They felt his teacher knew best the type of program Paul would need in order to succeed. After his teacher spoke to officials at the college, they felt confident his needs would be met.

Peterson's Colleges with Programs for Learning-Disabled Students is a good place to start a college search. It is available at most local libraries. Write to the individual colleges and ask for a list of their special education services. Remember, however, that a college is more than its special education department. Find a school that is right in terms of size, program, location, and cost. Once you have narrowed your choices to 5 to 10 schools, you can examine individual schools more closely for their services. Your school's guidance office or special education director can provide you with a list of questions related to your child's specific needs. The following list provides a good place to start.

1. Does the college offer a comprehensive LD program?

2. What types of support services are available? Where are they offered?

3. Who provides the support services? Are professional tutors available, or does the school rely on peer tutors? Are the tutors trained to work with students with learning disabilities?

4. Will the academic advisor be trained in the field of learning disabilities?

5. Is the regular academic staff available to provide extra help for learning disabled students?

6. Will the student need to seek help, or are support services scheduled into his program?

7. Is there communication between the special education staff and the regular staff? Are the professors familiar with special learning needs?

8. What counseling services are provided? Academic? Emotional? Career? How does the student arrange for these services?

9. What accommodations are made for learning disabled students? Are untimed tests an option? May they tape lectures? May they use books on tape? Are modifications made in requirements? Are oral examinations an option? Are notetakers and readers available? Are word processors/calculators available for student use?

10. What is the average class size? Are small study groups available for large lecture classes?

11. Are study skills courses available? May they be taken for credit?

12. Are special orientation programs offered for learning disabled students? Are summer programs offered?

13. Is there an organized self-help group for students with learning disabilities?

14. May learning disabled students carry a reduced course load? Will it affect their full-time status? Are waivers granted to LD students who cannot pass certain courses?

15. Are there special admission requirements for LD students? Are special applications required? Are SAT scores considered? Are untimed SAT results accepted?

16. Are there additional fees for special services? What is the cost?

Begin early. The process will be time-consuming and it may take a while to develop a list of schools with the programs you are looking for. You will want to visit the colleges your child is considering if possible. You can get a lot more information face-to-face than through a book or brochure. You can examine the attitudes of the staff and you can learn specifics about support services. This is a stressful time for all families, but it is also an exciting time.

A college student home for the summer told us, "It was hard because I had to do everything on my own. It was the most difficult thing I have ever done. But, as you can see, I made it."

Chapter 15

Understanding Your Rights and the Law

Paul and Jane were somewhat confused and concerned when they received notification that the school wanted to evaluate their five-year-old daughter Randi to determine if she had learning disabilities. Randi was their only child and they had never had any concerns about her learning. She was always eager to sit with them and listen to stories, and she played well with her friends. They felt threatened by the phone call.

They needed more information. Why did the school want to evaluate their daughter? What would happen if she did have a learning disability? How would that affect her education? Should they refuse to have her tested? Was that an option? Would their daughter have to leave school if they did not agree to have her evaluated?

They had dozens of questions. Without experience, they were not sure what the evaluation would entail and what difference it would make to them and to Randi in the long run. They were not sure what they stood to gain and what, if anything, they were giving up.

Once Jane and Paul had an opportunity to review the regulations governing special education evaluations and services available in their district, they felt much more confident that their feelings and concerns would be addressed. The information was readily available. All they needed to do was ask the special educational professionals in their school system to provide them with a copy of the regulations.

It is important for parents of children with learning disabilities to understand their basic rights. Without that information you cannot act effectively as your child's advocate. You are already speaking up for your child if you are working with schools, doctors, and other professionals on his behalf. You can be even more effective if you understand the law. You can be more confident that your child will get all of the services he needs. Knowing your rights and acting with that information does not mean that you will need to become an adversary of your child's school. This information will enable you to communicate with the school system effectively and to present your message through the proper channels and in the proper manner. It will help you know when to ask for services, how to ask, and whom to ask. Your involvement and knowledge can influence the future of services in your state.

The special education laws are also a vehicle for raising awareness about educational problems that affect an increasing number of children. The laws have helped make changes in the way children with learning disabilities are viewed. These children used to be thought of as underachievers. They were troublemakers, discipline problems, and class clowns. Many never graduated from high school. If they were boys, they might be sent off to military school.

For the majority of children who are learning disabled, the system works quite smoothly. The difficulty the child has can be remediated within a short period of time during the school day and dedicated teachers work closely with you to make sure this happens.

However, if your child does not fit into the programs available at his school, if you are not comfortable with the information you are receiving from the professionals, if you are unsure the services your child is receiving are actually meeting his needs, if the promised services are not actually being provided...if, if, if...you will feel more comfortable knowing about the law and your rights in providing for your child's education.

The many parents who have gone through this process before you have blazed a trail that is relatively easy to follow. They have formed associations to help you and provide you with support. (Listings of some of those associations are included in Appendices B and C of this book.) They offer courses and workshops on the law and your rights. Many of them have become professional advocates who will work with you and help you through the process if you do not feel that you want to, or are able to, go through it alone. Your child's evaluation coordinator will provide you with information about your rights, including information about other agencies you can contact if you feel that you are not getting what you want from the school district.

Your individual school system or your state department of education is an excellent source of information about the federal regulations governing the education of students with learning disabilities. They are the best source for current interpretations regarding the laws in your state. Check there for answers to specific questions.

We have included this brief overview to help you understand your rights under the federal law.

The Education of All Handicapped Children Act, also known as Public Law 94-142 (reauthorized and renamed the Individuals with Disabilities Education Act, or IDEA—Public Law 101-476) responded to this growing population of children who needed extra support. The idea of "learning disability" was defined, and specific guidelines and programs were developed to help these students succeed. Colleges also responded and created programs of study to educate teachers about ways to work with these children.

The main provisions of the federal law are explained here to provide you with a basic understanding of the intent. You can obtain a complete copy of it from your congressional representative or from your state department of education. The more you know about the law, the more comfortable you will be in working with your school system on your child's behalf.

1. The law states that *all* children with disabilities must be provided with a free and appropriate education. This education must provide special education and related services to meet the needs of these children. "Children with disabilities" includes those "with mental retardation, hearing impairments including deafness, speech or language impairments, visual impairments including blindness, serious emotional disturbance, orthopedic impairments, autism, traumatic brain injury, other health impairments or specific learning disabilities and who, by reason thereof need special education and related services."

The law further ensures that your child, between the ages of 3 and 21, will be educated at no cost to you, even if your local school district does not have a program that is right for him. If your city or town cannot educate your child within the school system, it will have to pay for a program in another city, town, collaborative, or private placement—whichever is most appropriate.

2. If you or your school staff suspects your child needs special education services, the following process must take place:

a. A referral is made by you or your child's teacher to the special education department of your child's school.

b. A preassessment conference between you and the special education coordinator of your child's school will be held before the assessment takes place. This provides you with an opportunity to find out what will take place during your child's assessment and to ask any questions you might have about the assessment or the special education services provided by the school system. You must consent, in writing, to the evaluation before it can take place.

c. Your child will be evaluated by a team of professionals who will look for specific strengths and weaknesses to determine if there is a need for special education services. Your child will be assessed in all areas related to the suspected disability. Assessments by your child's classroom teacher and by a specialist in the area of the suspected learning disability must be included. You may request assessments in areas that have not been recommended. These areas might include health, vision, hearing, social and emotional status, general intelligence, academic performance, communication skills, and motor abilities.

d. The tests administered must not be racially or culturally biased. They must also be in your child's native language.

e. No single evaluation or opinion will be the only factor in determining the need for special programs. The evaluation process must be a team process and the members of the team are determined by the specific needs of your child. You, the parent, must also be a part of that team and you must be involved in any decisions made regarding your child.

f. Within 45 school days the school must evaluate your child, conduct a team meeting, and develop an appropriate educational plan. The first 30 days are for the evaluation, and the next 15 days are for the meeting and writing the IEP. All professionals who conducted assessments of your child should be at this meeting. Each report should include specific strengths and weaknesses and recommendations for remediation, if necessary. If a special need is indicated, an Individual Educational Plan (IEP) will be written detailing the placement recommended and the services to be provided.

3. Each child serviced under this law must have an Individualized Educational Plan (IEP). This plan is developed at a meeting of the special education team that evaluated your child. You are a part of this team. You must be notified of this meeting early enough to ensure that you will be able to attend and it must be scheduled at a

mutually agreed upon time. You may also choose to bring anyone along with you who may make you feel more comfortable or who might help the entire team view your child as a whole person.

The IEP consists of very important information about your child. You, as a member of the team, provide valuable information necessary in developing the written plan. The plan will provide:

a. A profile of your child's strengths and weaknesses.

b. Important information about his medical or educational history

c. Current performance levels in all areas for which he will be receiving help.

d. Annual goals for progress based on his current performance level.

e. The methods and materials to be used to help him meet those goals.

f. Specific objectives that will be addressed during the time of the plan.

g. The amount of time your child will receive special education services.

h. The regular education classes your child will participate in.

i. The dates for the beginning and ending point of the services.

When you participate in this meeting, make sure you understand the words that are being used to describe your child. Professionals often use jargon most parents do not understand. They might not realize that you don't understand unless you say so. Don't be afraid to ask questions. You need to understand what everyone is saying so you can be comfortable with the decisions that are made.

Make sure you understand the IEP and agree with it, as this will be the working document used by your school's professionals to guide your child's educational progress. You have the right to accept or reject any or all of the services indicated or to request an independent evaluation.

If you accept the plan, your child will begin receiving the special education services described according to the timetable listed in the plan.

4. The criteria used for determining whether a child has a learning disability are specific. Your child's team may determine that your child has a specific learning disability if she is not able to learn at a level expected based on her age and ability. For example, if your first grade child can't keep up with the first graders in her class, she might need special services. Also, if the team finds that there is a large difference between your child's intelligence and her achievement in one or more of these areas—oral expression, listening comprehension, written expression, reading skills, reading comprehension, mathematics calculation, mathematic reasoning—she will be identified as a student with special needs.

5. Your child's special education services must be delivered in the least restrictive environment. This means that he must not be separated from nonhandicapped students unless the nature and severity of his handicap is such that "education in regular classes with the use of supplementary aids and services cannot be achieved satisfactorily." This decision is made at the IEP meeting described above. You want your child to have an opportunity, whenever possible, of being a part of the "normal" activities of the school. However, you also don't want him forced into impossible competition. Decisions about placement must be made carefully.

6. Each child who is receiving special education services must be reevaluated at least every three years. The reevaluation can take place more frequently if you or your child's teacher request it.

Your child's plan will be reviewed on an annual basis to ensure the program is still appropriate.

7. If you reject the plan, you have the right to a free, independent evaluation paid for by the school system. This evaluation must cover the same areas as the evaluation conducted by the school system. During the time that the independent evaluation is being conducted, your child must remain in his current educational placement.

8. You are entitled to due process under the law. You must be informed of all procedures you can follow to make sure your child gets the services she needs. You also have the right to an impartial "due process" hearing to try to settle any dispute between you and the school system. Decisions about your child's education cannot be made without notification to you or without your consent. Your consent is needed for each step of the evaluation and education process. Nothing can be done to or for your child without that consent. You must be notified when the school wants to evaluate or reevaluate your child, change your child's placement, suspend your child from school, or terminate the special education services.

You have the right to examine all records pertaining to your child.

9. All information about your child is kept confidential. It cannot be released to anyone else without your written consent.

10. The law also established early intervention programs for children with developmental delays between birth to age three. An amendment in 1991 expanded these services to include children between the ages of three to five who experience, or are at risk for, developmental delays. If you are concerned about your infant or toddler, contact your local school system to get further information about these services.

If all of this makes you feel overwhelmed, you are not alone. The paperwork alone sometimes frightens parents and makes them wonder why they need so much "protection" from the school. Remember, both you and the school have the best interest of your child uppermost in your minds. Work closely, in partnership, with the school to ensure that your child receives the special education services he needs in order to maximize his potential. Today's laws protect you and your child. A working knowledge of these laws will help you and your school system develop an appropriate plan to provide your child with a good education and to enable him to become a positive participant in society.

Chapter 16

Understanding the Jargon

A Glossary of Terms Commonly Used in Special Education Evaluations and Team Meetings

Advocate - A person who can help you through the special education maze and can help protect your rights. You might hire a professional advocate if you disagree with the findings of the school system and want a program for your child that is different from the one the school is offering. Often other parents who are more familiar with the special education system might be willing to accompany you to meetings and function in the role of advocate.

Annual Review - A yearly meeting to evaluate the effectiveness of a special education program and to determine whether it continues to work or if it should be modified.

Appeal - A legal process in which you request a hearing when you have a disagreement with the school system over your child's educational plan.

Articulation - The production of speech sounds and words.

Assessment - A test to determine the need for special education services.

Attention deficit disorder (ADD) - An inability to maintain focus and attention on a task.

Attention deficit hyperactivity disorder (ADHD) - An inability to maintain focus and attention on a task accompanied by excessive movement. See *hyperactivity*.

Attention span - The amount of time a child can stay with a certain task.

Auditory discrimination - The ability to recognize differences between different sounds and words, such as *pet* and *pat; pam* and *pan.*

Auditory processing - Understanding and integrating spoken information, words, or sounds. This is different from the actual ability to hear.

Automatization - Quick recall and use of information.

Behavior modification - A technique used to encourage positive actions through rewards and to discourage negative actions by ignoring them.

Child study team (CST) - A preferral team which develops classroom modifications in an effort to prevent the necessity of a special education evaluation.

Chunking - Breaking down information into small and meaningful contexts in order to remember it.

Classification - A label necessary in many states for a child to receive special education services.

Cognitive ability - A child's capacity for learning, which is related to his level of intelligence.

Communication - The ability to pass information to another person, either by speaking or writing or through gestures and body language.

Compensation - Using a strong ability to cover or mask a weak one. For example, a child might use a calculator for math facts because he has a memory problem or use a typewriter because of poor handwriting.

Cylert - The trade name of one of several stimulant-type drugs used to modify hyperactivity.

Deficit - An area of difficulty that interferes with a child's learning.

Developmental delay - A lag in mental or physical development.

Dexedrine - The trade name of one of several stimulant-type drugs used to modify hyperactivity.

Discrepancy - A significant difference or inconsistency.

Distractibility - The inability to attend to a task due to noises, sights, or thoughts.

Dyscalculia - Extreme difficulty in performing math skills.

Dysgraphia - Extreme difficulty in writing.

Dyslexia - Extreme difficulty in learning to read.

Early intervention - The identification and education of a preschool child (before the age of three) who has a handicapping condition or is at risk of developing a handicapping condition.

Evaluation - A group of tests that determine the way in which a child learns best.

Expressive language - The ability to communicate with others by speaking, writing, and/or gestures.

Eye-hand coordination - The process of using eyes and hands together to perform a task.

Fine motor control - The coordination of the smaller muscles of the body, particularly those of the hands, to make precise movements as in writing or manipulating puzzles, peg boards, and other small objects.

Free appropriate public education - As defined by the United States Public Law 94-142, it means "special education and related services which are provided at public expense, under public supervision and direction and without charge...and are provided in conformity with an individualized education program." In other words, a child must be educated in a way that takes into account his special learning needs, at no cost to parents.

Gross motor control - The coordination of the large muscles, particularly those used for walking, running, and sitting. Difficulties in this area might affect posture in class and could have an impact on writing.

Hyperactivity - Excessive and almost constant motion that impairs a child's ability to learn.

Impulsivity - The tendency to act or speak quickly without thinking about the meaning or consequences of such actions or words.

Independent evaluation - Additional testing conducted by one or more qualified examiners not employed by the school system, identical to the type of testing done by the school. This type of testing is done when parents disagree with recommendations made by the school evaluators, or when they desire a second opinion.

Individualized Education Plan (IEP) - The document prepared by an evaluation team that details strengths and weaknesses and the specific areas in which a student will receive special help.

Inversions - Confusion in the vertical direction of numbers or letters, for example *6* for *9*, *m* for *w*.

Kinesthetic - Involving muscular responses and sense of touch. Kinesthetic approaches to learning include, for example, teaching a child prereading skills with sandpaper letters that she can trace with her fingers.

Learning disability - A disorder in one or more of the educational processes that causes extreme difficulty in listening, thinking, speaking, reading, writing, spelling, and/or calculating.

Least restrictive environment - An educational program that allows a child to be educated, to the greatest extent possible, with students who do not need special education services.

Mainstreaming - The inclusion of special education students in regular education classes. This may involve having them participate in art, music, and gym classes only, or may include having them in academic classes as well. See *least restrictive environment.*

Manipulatives - Anything a child can touch and move to help him understand math concepts. For example, he might use sticks or buttons to help him with counting and combining numbers.

Modality - The way in which information is taken in by a child's senses. Specialists often refer to the *visual, auditory* or *kinesthetic modalities* and make determinations as to which modality (sight, sound, touch) is a strength or weakness for a child.

Motor memory - The ability to remember how to perform specific motor tasks, those involving muscle and movement, such as the formation of letters for writing or the actions involved in washing hands or brushing hair.

Motor planning - Movements, planned in the brain, to organize, sequence, and carry out unfamiliar actions.

Multisensory - The use of more than one sense (sight, sound, or touch) to obtain information.

Neurological evaluation - Tests to determine if certain problems are caused by difficulties within the nervous system.

Perception - The process of taking in information through the senses and interpreting and organizing the information.

Phonetic approach - A method of teaching reading by teaching the individual sounds that are combined to make up words.

Prereferral - A meeting to develop strategies to address a child's difficulties in school. This could prevent the need for a special education referral.

Profile - The section of an educational plan that states a student's specific strengths and weaknesses, any physical constraints, how she receives and expresses information, her current performance level, and other information relevant to her unique learning style.

Prototype - Some states use a classification system that states how much time a student will receive special education services outside of his regular classroom.

Psychological tests - Evaluations given by a certified psychologist that measure intelligence and identify emotional issues.

Public Law (PL) 94-142 - The federal law that requires each state to provide a free and appropriate education to children with disabilities.

Receptive language - The taking in of language that is communicated by others either in writing, speaking, or through body language; understanding of the language a child hears and/or reads.

Reevaluation - An evaluation of a student conducted every three years while he is receiving special education services. The purpose of the reevaluation is to determine if a child is still in need of current services and if new services are necessary.

Referral - The beginning of a formal evaluation process. All children must be referred to special education (by a parent, guardian, or teacher) in order for testing to begin.

Related services - Any services, in addition to special education services, necessary to ensure that a student can benefit from special education. These might include transportation, specific therapies, and medical services.

Resource room - A place outside the classroom setting where a student receives special education services.

Reversal - Writing or reading numbers in mirror image. For example, writing or reading a *d* for a *b* or a *p* for a *q*.

Ritalin - The trade name of one of several stimulant-type drugs used to modify hyperactivity.

Screening - A brief look at a child by special education professionals to determine if there is a need for a full evaluation.

Self-monitoring - The ability of a student to notice any mistakes he makes and to correct them on his own.

Sensory integration (SI) - The ability of a student to organize the information she receives through her senses so that she can respond appropriately.

Sequencing - Processing information in the correct order in which it was received. For example, your phone number is only correct when it is dialed in the correct sequence.

Spatial organization - Using space in an orderly and meaningful way.

Special education - Specifically designed instruction to meet the unique needs of a child if he is not able to learn in a regular classroom, or if he requires special work in addition to regular classroom activities in order to succeed.

Spiral back - To continually reteach previously covered materials in an effort to ensure learning.

Tactile - The use of touch to help a student understand concepts. She might need to touch sandpaper letters in order to remember them, for example.

Transposition - Confusing the order of letters in words or numerals in numbers. For example, reading *girl* as *gril* or *saw* as *was*, *325* as *523*.

Visual processing - Taking in, understanding, remembering, and using information received through the eyes.

Visual-motor integration - A student's ability to translate what he sees into a physical action. This would apply to copying letters, numbers, and objects.

Word retrieval - The ability of a student to remember and appropriately use a specific word.

Appendix A

State Directors of Special Education

State-by-state listings of state directors of special education are maintained by the National Association of State Directors of Special Education. The people who hold these positions may change, but the department addresses and phone numbers should remain constant. Contact these offices if you need specific information about the special education services in a particular state.

ALABAMA

Dr. Bill East, Assistant Director
Alabama Department of Education
Division of Special Education Services
50 N. Ripley (Gordon Persons Building)
Montgomery, AL 36130-3901
(205) 242-8114

ALASKA

Dr. Richard Smiley, Acting Director
Office for Special and Supplemental Services
Alaska Department of Education
P.O. Box F
Juneau, AK 99811
(907) 465-2970

AMERICAN SAMOA

Ms. Jane French, Director
Special Education
Department of Education
Pago Pago, American Samoa 96799
(684) 633-1323

ARIZONA

Dr. Kathryn A. Lund, Deputy
Associate Superintendent, Special
Education
Arizona Department of Education
1535 W. Jefferson
Phoenix, AZ 85007-3280
(602) 542-3084

ARKANSAS

Dr. Diane Sydoriak, Associate
Director of Special Education
Department of Education Building
Room 105-C
#4 State Capitol Mall
Little Rock, AR 72201-1071
(501) 682-4221

CALIFORNIA

Dr. Leo Sandoval, Acting State
Director Special Education
California Department of Education
721 Capitol Mall
Sacramento, CA 95814
(916) 657-3567

COLORADO

Dr. Fred Smokoski, Director
Special Education Services Unit
Colorado Department of Education
201 E. Colfax
Denver, CO 80203
(303) 866-6695

CONNECTICUT

Dr. Tom Gillung, Bureau Chief
Bureau of Special Education and
Pupil Personnel Services
Connecticut Department of
Education
25 Industrial Park Rd.
Middletown, CT 06457
(203) 638-4265

DELAWARE

Dr. Carl M. Haltom, State Director
Division For Exceptional Children
Department of Public Instruction
P.O. Box 1402
Dover, DE 19903-1402
(302) 739-5471

DISTRICT OF COLUMBIA

Dr. Doris Woodson, Assistant
Superintendent
Division of Special Education and
Pupil Personnel Services
D.C. Public Schools
Webster Administration Building
10th & H Streets NW
Washington, DC 20001
(202) 724-4178

FLORIDA

Mrs. Bettye Weir, Bureau Chief
Bureau for Education Exceptional Students
Florida Education Center
325 W. Gaines Street
Suite 614
Tallahassee, FL 32399-0400
(904) 488-1570

GEORGIA

Dr. Joan Jordan, Director
Division for Exceptional Children
Georgia Department of Education
1952 Twin Towers East
205 Butler Street
Atlanta, GA 39334-5040
(404) 656-3963

GUAM

Dr. Steve L. Spencer, Associate Superintendent
Department of Education
Special Education Division
P.O. Box DE
Agana, Guam 96910
(671) 646-1416

HAWAII

Dr. Margaret Donovan, State Administrator
Hawaii Department of Education
Special Education Section
3430 Leahi Avenue
Honolulu, HI 96815
(808) 737-3720

IDAHO

Mr. Fred Balcom, Supervisor
Special Education Section
State Department of Education
650 W. State Street
Boise, ID 83720-3650
(208) 334-3940

ILLINOIS

Ms. Gail Lieberman, Assistant Superintendent
Department of Special Education
Illinois State Board of Education
Mail Code E-216
100 N. First Street
Springfield, IL 62777-0001
(217) 782-6601

INDIANA

Mr. Paul Ash, State Director
Division of Special Education
Indiana Department of Education
Room 229 State House
Indianapolis, IN 46204-2798
(317) 232-0570

IOWA

Mr. Frank Vance, Chief
Bureau of Special Education
Iowa Department of Public Instruction
Grimes State Office Building
Des Moines, IA 50319-0146
(515) 281-3176

KANSAS

Ms. Betty Weithers, Team Leader
Special Education Outcomes Team
Kansas State Department of Education
120 S.E. Tenth Avenue
Topeka, KS 66612-1182
(913) 296-3869

KENTUCKY

Dr. Theodore R. Drain, Director
Kentucky Department of Education
Division of Exceptional Children Services
500 Mero Street, Room 805
Frankfort, KY 40601
(502) 564-4970

LOUISIANA

Dr. Tama Luther, Acting Director
Louisiana Department of Education
Office of Special Education Services
P.O. Box 94064
9th Floor
Baton Rouge, LA 70804-9064
(504) 342-3633

MAINE

Mr. David Noble Stockford, Director
Division of Special Education
Maine Department of Education & Cultural Services
Station #23
Augusta, ME 04333
(207) 289-5953

MARYLAND

Mr. Richard Steinke, State Director
Maryland Department of Education
Division of Special Education
200 W. Baltimore Street
Baltimore, MD 21021-2595
(301) 333-2490

MASSACHUSETTS

Dr. Mary Beth Fafard, Associate Commissioner
Division of Special Education
Department of Education
1385 Hancock Street
3rd Floor
Quincy, MA 02169-5183
(617) 770-7468

MICHIGAN

Dr. Richard Baldwin, State Director
Special Education Services
Michigan Department of Education
P.O. Box 30008
Lansing, MI 48909-7508
(517) 373-9433

MINNESOTA

Mr. Wayne Erickson, Manager
Special Education Section
Department of Education
812 Capitol Square Building
550 Cedar Street
St. Paul, MN 55101-2233
(612) 296-1793

MISSISSIPPI

Ms. Carolyn Black, Bureau Director
Bureau of Special Services
State Department of Education
P.O. Box 771
Jackson, MS 39205-0771
(601) 359-3490

MISSOURI

Dr. John B. Heskett, Coordinator
Special Education Programs
Department of Elementary and
Secondary Education
P.O. Box 480
Jefferson City, MO 65102-0480
(314) 751-2965

MONTANA

Mr. Robert Runkel, Director
Division of Special Education
Office of Public Instruction
State Capitol
Room 106
Helena, MT 59620
(406) 444-4429

NEBRASKA

Mr. Gary M. Sherman, Director
Special Education Office
Nebraska Department of Education
301 Centennial Mall South
Box 94987
Lincoln, NE 68509-4987
(402) 471-2471

NEVADA

Ms. Gloria Dopf, Director
Special Education Branch
Nevada Department of Education
Capitol Complex
440 W. King Street
Carson City, NV 89710-0004
(702) 687-3140

NEW HAMPSHIRE

Mr. Robert T. Kennedy, Director
Bureau for Special Education
Services
New Hampshire Department of
Education
101 Pleasant Street
Concord, NH 03301-3860
(603) 271-3741

NEW JERSEY

Dr. Jeffrey V. Osowski, Director
Division of Special Education
New Jersey Department of
Education
P.O. Box CN 500
225 W. State Street
Trenton, NJ 08625-0001
(609) 633-6833

NEW MEXICO

Dr. Linda M. Wilson, State Director
Special Education
State Department of Education
300 Don Gaspar Avenue
Sante Fe, NM 87501-2786
(505) 827-6541

NEW YORK

Mr. Tom Neveldine, Assistant Commissioner
Office for Special Education Services
New York State Education Department
Room 1073
Education Building Annex
Albany, NY 12234-0001
(518) 474-5548

NORTH CAROLINA

Mr. Lowell Harris, Director
Division of Exceptional Children's Services
North Carolina Department of Public Instruction
116 W. Edenton
Education Building #442
Raleigh, NC 27603-1712
(919) 733-3921

NORTH DAKOTA

Dr. Gary W. Gronberg, Director
Special Education
Department of Public Instruction
600 E. Boulevard
Bismarck, ND 58505-0440
(701) 224-2277

OHIO

Mr. John Herner, Director
Division of Special Education
Ohio Department of Education
933 High Street
Worthington, OH 43085-4087
(614) 466-2650

OKLAHOMA

Mr. John Corpolongo
Executive Director, Special Education Section
State Department of Education
2500 N. Lincoln Boulevard
Oklahoma City, OK 73105-4599
(405) 521-3351

OREGON

Dr. Karen Brazeau, Associate Superintendent
Special Education and Student Services Division
Oregon Department of Education
700 Pringle Parkway SE
Salem, OR 97310-0290
(503) 378-3598

PENNSYLVANIA

Dr. James Tucker, Director
Bureau of Special Education
Pennsylvania Department of Education
333 Market Street
Harrisburg, PA 17126-0333
(717) 783-6913

PUERTO RICO

Dr. Cesar D. Vazquez
Assistant Secretary of Special Education
Department of Education
P.O. Box 759
San Juan, PR 00919-0759
(809) 759-7228

RHODE ISLAND

Mr. Robert M. Pryhoda, Coordinator
Department of Education/Special Education Programs
Roger Williams Building
Room 209
22 Hayes Street
Providence, RI 02908-5025
(401) 277-3505

SOUTH CAROLINA

Dr. Ora Spann, State Director
Office of Programs for Exceptional Children
State Department of Education
Room 505
Rutledge Building, 1429 Senate
Columbia, SC 29201
(803) 734-8353

SOUTH DAKOTA

Ms. Deborah Barnett
Office of Special Education
Department of Education & Cultural Affairs
700 Governor's Drive
Pierre, SD 57501-2291
(605) 773-3315

TENNESSEE

Mr. Joseph Fisher, Associate Commissioner
Special Education Programs
Tennessee Department of Education
132 Cordell Hull Building
Nashville, TN 37219
(615) 741-2851

TEXAS

Ms. Jill Gray, Senior Director
Special Education Unit
Texas Education Agency
W. B. Travis Building
Room 5-120
1701 N. Congress Avenue
Austin, TX 78701-2486
(512) 463-9414

UTAH

Dr. Steve Kukic, Director of At Risk & Special Education Services
Special Education Services Unit
Utah State Office of Education
250 E. 500 South
Salt Lake City, UT 84111-3204
(801) 538-7706

VERMONT

Mr. Dennis Kane, Acting Director
Division of Special Education
State Office Building
120 State Street
Montpelier, VT 05602-3403
(802) 828-3141

VIRGIN ISLANDS

Mrs. Priscilla I. Stridiron
State Director, Special Education
Department of Education
P.O. Box 6640
Charlotte Amalie
St. Thomas, Virgin Islands 00801
(809) 776-5802

VIRGINIA

Dr. Austin Tuning, Lead Specialist for Special Education
Division of Pre & Early Adolescent Education
Virginia Department of Education
P.O. Box 6Q
Richmond, VA 23216-2060
(804) 225-2847

WASHINGTON

Dr. Douglas Gill, State Director
Special Education Section
Superintendent of Public Instruction
Old Capital Building
Olympia, WA 98504-0001
(206) 753-6733

WEST VIRGINIA

Ms. Nancy J. Thabet, Director
Office of Special Education
West Virginia Department of Education
Building #6
Room B-304 Capitol Complex
Charleston, WV 25305
(304) 558-2696

WISCONSIN

Ms. Juanita S. Pawlisch, Assistant Superintendent
Department of Public Instruction
Division of Handicapped Children and Pupil Services
125 S. Webster
P.O. Box 7841
Madison, WI 53707-7841
(608) 266-1649

WYOMING

Ms. Margie Simineo, State Director
Special Education Unit
Wyoming Department of Education
Hathaway Building
2nd Floor
2300 Capitol Avenue
Cheyenne, WY 82002-0050
(307) 777-7417

Appendix B

Parent Training and Information Programs

This listing includes groups that provide technical assistance, training, and referral information for parents. Contact the groups in your state for more specific information about their services.

ALABAMA

Carol Blades
Special Education Action Committee, Inc. (SEAC)
P.O. Box 161274
Mobile, AL 36616-2274
(205) 478-1208

ALASKA

Jenny Weaver
Alaska PARENTS Resource Center
P.O. Box 32198
Juneau, AK 99803
(907) 790-2246

ARIZONA

Mary Slaughter
Judie Walker
Pilot Parent Partnerships
2150 E. Highland Avenue
Phoenix, AZ 85016
(602) 468-3001

ARKANSAS

Bonnie Johnson
Arkansas Disability Coalition
10002 W. Markham
Suite B-7
Little Rock, AR 72205
(501) 221-1330

Barbara Semrau
FOCUS, Inc.
2917 King Street
Suite C
Jonesboro, AR 72401
(501) 935-2750

CALIFORNIA

Joan Tellefsen
TASK
100 W. Cerritos Avenue
Anaheim, CA 92805-6546
(714) 533-8275

Florene Poyadue
Parents Helping Parents
535 Race Street
Suite 220
San Jose, CA 95126
(408) 288-5010

Pam Steneberg
DREDF
2212 6th Street
Berkeley, CA 94710
(510) 644-2555

Joan Kilburn
Matrix, A Parent Network and Resource Center
P.O. Box 6541
San Rafael, CA 94903
(415) 499-3877

Marion Karian
Exceptional Parents Unlimited
4120 N. First Street
Fresno, CA 93726
(209) 229-2000

COLORADO

Judy Martz
Barbara Buswell
PEAK Parent Center, Inc.
6055 Lehman Drive
Suite 101
Colorado Springs, CO 80918
(719) 531-9400

CONNECTICUT

Nancy Prescott
CT Parent Advocacy Center, Inc. (CPAC)
P.O. Box 579
East Lyme, CT 06333
(203) 739-3089

DELAWARE

Marie-Anne Aghazadian
PIC of Delaware, Inc.
700 Barksdale Road
Suite 6
Newark, DE 19711
(302) 366-0152

DISTRICT OF COLUMBIA

Charlene Howard
COPE
P.O. Box 90498
Washington, DC 20090-0498
(202) 526-6814

FLORIDA

Janet Jacoby
Florida PEN
5510 Gray Street
Suite 220
Tampa, FL 33609
(813) 289-1122

GEORGIA

Patty Webb
Parents Educating Parents (PEP)
Georgia ARC
1851 Ram Runway
Suite 104
College Park, GA 30337-2615
(404) 761-3150

HAWAII

Kathy Gould
Susan Klopotek
AWARE/Learning Disabilities Association of Hawaii (LDAH)
200 N. Vineyard Blvd.
Suite 103
Honolulu, HI 96817
(808) 536-9684

IDAHO

Debra Johnson
Idaho Parents UNLTD, Inc.
Parent Education Resource Center
4696 Overland Road
Suite 478
Boise, ID 83704
(208) 342-5884

ILLINOIS

Charlotte Des Jardins
Family Resource Center on Disabilities (FRCD)
20 E. Jackson Boulevard
Room 900
Chicago, IL 60604
(312) 939-3513

Donald Moore
Designs for Change
220 S. State Street
Room 1900
Chicago, IL 60604
(312) 922-0317

INDIANA

Richard Burden
Indiana Resource Center for Families with Special Needs (IN*SOURCE)
833 Northside Boulevard
Building No. 1, Rear
South Bend, IN 46617
(219) 234-7101

IOWA

Carla Lawson
Iowa Exceptional Parents Center (IEPC)
33 N. 12th Street
P.O. Box 1151
Fort Dodge, IA 50501
(515) 576-5870

KANSAS

Patricia Gerdel
Families Together, Inc.
1023 S.W. Gage Street
Topeka, KS 66604
(913) 273-6343

KENTUCKY

Paulette Logsdon
Kentucky Special Parent Involvement Network (KY-SPIN)
2210 Goldsmith Lane
Suite 118
Louisville, KY 40218
(502) 456-0923

LOUISIANA

Debbie Braud
Rose Gilbert
Programs of Families Helping Families of Greater New Orleans–Project PROMPT
4323 Division Street
Suite 110
Metairie, LA 70002-3179
(504) 888-9111

MAINE

Janice LaChance
Margaret Squires
Special Needs Parent Information Network (SPIN)
P.O. Box 2067
Augusta, ME 04338
(207) 582-2504

MARYLAND

Cory Moore
Parents Place of MD, Inc.
7257 Parkway Drive
Suite 210
Hanover, MD 21076
(410) 712-0900

MASSACHUSETTS

Artie Higgins
Federation for Children with Special Needs
95 Berkeley Street
Suite 104
Boston, MA 02116
(617) 482-2915

MICHIGAN

Barbara Cardinal
Martha Wilson
Parents Are Experts: Parents Training Parents Project UCP of Metropolitan Detroit, Inc.
23077 Greenfield Road
Suite 205
Southfield, MI 48075
(313) 557-5070

Sue Pratt
Citizens Alliance to Uphold Special Education (CAUSE)
313 S. Washington Square, LL
Lansing, MI 48933
(517) 485-4084

MINNESOTA

Marge Goldberg
Paula F. Goldberg
PACER Center, Inc.
4826 Chicago Avenue South
Minneapolis, MN 55417
(612) 827-2966

MISSISSIPPI

Ginger Smith
Association of Developmental Organizations of Mississippi ADOM/MSPAC
332 New Market Drive
Jackson, MS 39209
(601) 922-3210

MISSOURI

Marianne Toombs, Director
Missouri Parents Act (MPACT)
1722 W. South Glenstone, #125
Springfield, MO 65804
(417) 882-7434

Beth Mollenkamp
625 N. Euclid, #405
St. Louis, MO 63108
(314) 361-1660

Carolyn Stewart
1115 E. 65th Street
Kansas City, MO 64131
(816) 333-6833

MONTANA

Katharin Kelker
Parents Let's Unite for Kids
EMC/SPED Building
Room 267
1500 N. 30th Street
Billings, MT 59101-0298
(406) 657-2055

NEBRASKA

Jean Sigler
NE Parents' Information Training Center
3610 Dodge Street
Omaha, NE 68131
(402) 346-0525

NEVADA

Bruce McAnnany
Charlene Rogerson
NTC Parent Connection
2860 E. Flamingo, Suite A
Las Vegas, NV 89121-2922
(702) 735-2922

NEW HAMPSHIRE

Judith Raskin
Parent Information Center
151-A Manchester Street
P.O. Box 1422
Concord, NH 03302
(603) 224-6299

NEW JERSEY

Diana Cuthbertson
Statewide Parent Advocacy Network, Inc. (SPAN)
516 North Avenue
East Westfield, NJ 07090
(908) 654-7726

NEW MEXICO

Paul Kline
EPICS Project
P.O. Box 788
Bernalillo, NM 87004
(505) 867-3396

Linda Coleman
Duane Edwards
Parents Reaching Out
1127 University Blvd.
Albuquerque, NM 87102
(505) 842-9045

NEW YORK

Joan M. Watkins
Parent Network Center (PNC)
1443 Main Street
Buffalo, NY 14209
(716) 885-1004

Director
Advocates for Children of New York, Inc.
24-16 Bridge Plaza South
Long Island City, NY 11101
(718) 729-8866

Karen Schlesinger
Resources for Children with Special Needs
200 Park Avenue South
Suite 816
New York, NY 10003
(212) 677-4650

NORTH CAROLINA

Connie Hawkins
Exceptional Children's Assistance Center (ECAC)
P.O. Box 16
Davidson, NC 28036
(704) 892-1321

Brenda Patton
Families First Coalition, Inc.
300 Enola Road
Morgantown, NC 28655
(704) 433-2782

NORTH DAKOTA

Kathryn Erickson
Pathfinder Services of North Dakota, Inc.
Pathfinder Parent Center
16th Street & 2nd Avenue SW
Minot, ND 58701
(701) 852-9426

OHIO

Cathy Heizman
Child Advocacy Center
1821 Summit Road
Suite 303
Cincinnati, OH 45237
(513) 821-2400

Margaret Burley
Ohio Coalition for the Education of Handicapped Children
1299 Campbell Road, Suite B
Marion, OH 43302
(614) 382-5452

Training Center
933 High Street
Suite 106
Worthington, OH 43085
(614) 431-1307

OKLAHOMA

Sharon Bishop
PRO-Oklahoma
1917 S. Harvard Avenue
Oklahoma City, OK 73128
(405) 681-9710

OREGON

Cheron Mayhall
Oregon COPE Project, Inc.
999 Locust Street, NE Box B
Salem, OR 97303
(503) 373-7477

PALAU

Philomina Milong
Palau Parent Network
P.O. Box 1583
Koror, Republic of Palau 76740
(608) 488-3513

PENNSYLVANIA

Christine Davis
Parents Union for Public Schools
311 S. Juniper Street
Suite 602
Philadelphia, PA 19107
(215) 546-1166

Gail Walker
Mentor Parent Program
Route 257, Salina Road
P.O. Box 718
Seneca, PA 16346
(814) 676-8615

Louise Thieme
Parent Education Network
333 E. 7th Avenue
York, PA 17404
(717) 845-9722

PUERTO RICO

Carmen Selles Vila
Asociacion De Padres Pro Biene Star
Ninos con Impedimento de PR, Inc.
P.O. Box 21301
Rio Piedras, PR 00928-1301
(809) 763-4665

RHODE ISLAND

Peter Gillis
Rhode Island Parent Information Network
Independence Square
500 Prospect Street
Pawtucket, RI 02860
(401) 727-4145

SOUTH CAROLINA

Colleen Lee
PRO-PARENTS
2712 Middleburg Drive
Suite 102
Columbia, SC 29204
(803) 779-3859

SOUTH DAKOTA

Monica Degen
South Dakota Parent Connection
P.O. Box 84813
Sioux Falls, SD 57118-4813
(605) 335-8844

TENNESSEE

Carol Westlake
Support and Training for Exceptional Parents (STEP)
1805 Hayes Street
Suite 100
Nashville, TN 37203
(615) 327-0294

TEXAS

Janice Foreman
Partners Resource Network
PATH
227 N. 18th Street, #2
Beaumont, TX 77707-2203
(409) 866-4726

Anita Mendez
Project PODER–Texas Fiesta Education
1226 N.W. 18th Street
San Antonio, TX 78207
(512) 732-8247

Agnes A. Johnson
Special Kids, Inc.
P.O. Box 61628
Houston, TX 77208-1628
(713) 643-9576

UTAH

Helen W. Post
Utah PIC
2290 E. 4500 South
Suite 110
Salt Lake City, UT 84117
(801) 272-1051

VERMONT

Connie Curtin
Vermont Parent Information Center
Network, Vermont/ARC
37 Champlain Mill
Winooski, VT 05404
(802) 655-4016

VIRGINIA

Dee Hayden
Parent Education Advocacy Training Center (PEATC)
228 S. Pitt Street, Room 300
Alexandria, VA 22314
(703) 836-2953

WASHINGTON

Martha Gentili
Washington PAVE
6316 S. 12th Street
Tacoma, WA 98465
(206) 565-2266

Heather Hebdon
PAVE/STOMP
Specialized Training of Military Parents
12208 Pacific Highway SW
Tacoma, WA 98499
(206) 588-1741

Joe Garcia
A Touchstones Program
6721 51st Avenue South
Seattle, WA 98118
(206) 721-0867

WEST VIRGINIA

Pat Haberbosch
W. Virginia PTI
Schroath Professional Building
2nd Floor, Suite 2-1
229 Washington Avenue
Clarksburgh, WV 26301
(304) 624-1436

WISCONSIN

Jan Serak/Charlotte Price
Parent Education Project
2001 W. Vliet Street
Milwaukee, WI 53205
(414) 937-8380

WYOMING

Terri Dawson
Wyoming PIC
5 N. Lobban
Buffalo, WY 82834
(307) 684-2277

Appendix C

Resource Organizations

Following is a listing of resources related to specific learning disabilities. Inclusion in this list does not suggest an endorsement of an organization or agency. Please contact the agency yourself to determine if the services offered can be of help to you and your child. Your involvement with one or more of these organizations can provide you with needed support and enable you to be a more effective advocate for your child.

American Council on Rural Special Education (ACRES)
National Rural Development Institute
Western Washington University
Miller Hall 359
Bellingham, WA 98225
(206) 676-3576

Services: Members of this organization work toward improving special education services for students with disabilities living in rural areas.

American Speech-Language-Hearing Association (ASHA)
10801 Rockville Pike
Rockville, MD 20852
(301) 897-5700 (Voice/TDD)
(800) 638-8255

Services: ASHA provides information about communication disorders. An information and referral service is available through their 800 number. The organization distributes the following directories for a fee:

"Directory of Educational Facilities for Learning Disabled Students"

"List of Colleges/Universities That Accept Students with Learning Disabilities"

"Summer Camp Directory for Children with Learning Disabilities"

Children with Attention Deficit Disorders (CHADD)
499 N.W. 70th Avenue
Suite 308
Plantation, FL 33317
(305) 587-3700

Services: This is a membership organization that offers information and support to parents and professionals. They publish a magazine, *Chadder*, twice yearly and a newsletter, *Chadder-Box*, six to eight times yearly with information about ADD. They sponsor support groups across the country.

Clearinghouse on Disability Information
Office of Special Education and Rehabilitative Services
U.S. Department of Education
Room 3132
Switzer Building
Washington, DC 20202
(202) 732-1241
(202) 732-1723

Services: The clearinghouse distributes information on federal funding for programs providing services for people with disabilities. It has information on a wide variety of topics related to specific disabilities and can refer people to appropriate sources for information.

The Council for Exceptional Children (CEC)
1920 Association Drive
Reston, VA 22091
(703) 620-3660

Services: This membership organization provides information about all handicapping conditions. They maintain a database of information about policies and research. They also publish information regarding specific aspects of special education. They publish two journals, *Teaching Exceptional Children* and *Exceptional Children*, available to members or by subscription without membership.

Disability Rights Education and Defense Fund (DREDF)
2212 Sixth Street
Berkeley, CA 94710
(415) 644-2555 (Voice/TDD)
(415) 841-8645

Services: DREDF works toward promoting the rights of people with disabilities. They work on civil rights legislation for people with disabilities and are a resource for information in the area of rights.

Dyslexia Research Institute, Inc.
4745 Centerville Road
Tallahassee, FL 32308
(904) 893-2216

Services: This is a national group that offers resources, services, and support to parents and professionals. They provide educational, testing, and counseling services as well as publications. They conduct training for teachers and parents nationally and consult around issues of advocacy and support groups. You can write them for a mailing list for information about dyslexia and ADD.

Educators Publishing Service, Inc.
75 Moulton Street
Cambridge, MA 02238
(617) 547-6706

Services: This company mainly publishes materials for schools, but they also have materials that are appropriate for individual tutoring in specific areas.

The Feingold Association of the United States (FAUS)
P.O. Box 6550
Alexandria, VA 22306
(703) 768-FAUS
(800) 321-FAUS

Services: This nonprofit parent organization assists parents of children with attention deficit disorder to help determine if food allergies might be the cause of the child's problem.

Gesell Institute of Human Development
310 Prospect Street
New Haven, CT 06511
(203) 777-3481

Services: The institute offers workshops and information to promote their philosophy of grouping children according to behavioral maturation rather than chronological age. They also refer parents to other professionals who might provide them with information about specific disabilities.

Learning Disabilities Association of America (LDA)
4156 Library Road
Pittsburgh, PA 15234
(412) 341-1515
(412) 341-8077

Services: This is a membership organization consisting of professionals and parents who work on advancing the education and lives of adults and children with learning disabilities. It serves as a national information center and provides a referral service. The organization deals with and provides information on all types of learning disabilities. They sponsor a national conference every year and publish a newsletter six times a year. You may write for a free sample copy of their newsletter, *Newsbriefs*.

National Association for Hearing and Speech Action (NAHSA)
10801 Rockville Pike
Rockville, MD 20852
(301) 897-8682 (Voice/TDD)
(800) 638-8255 (Voice/TDD)

Services: This is the consumer branch of the American Speech and Hearing Association. They provide information and a referral service.

National Association of Private Schools for Exceptional Children (NAPSEC)
1522 K Street NW
Suite 1032
Washington, DC 20005
(202) 408-3338

Services: This is a referral service that provides publications and conferences for people interested in private special education facilities.

National Center for Learning Disabilities (NCLD)
99 Park Avenue
New York, NY 10016
(212) 687-7211

Services: The center provides information on learning disabilities and is involved in increasing public awareness of LD. They publish a magazine, *Their World*, which provides articles of interest on learning disabilities.

National Center for Stuttering (NCS)
200 East 33rd Street
New York, NY 10017
(800) 221-2483

Services: This center uses a specialized method of treatment, called the air-flow technique, designed to address the physical aspects of stuttering. Brochures and books about this technique are available.

National Information Center for Children and Youth with Disabilities (NICHCY)
P.O. Box 1492
Washington, DC 20013
(800) 999-5599
(703) 893-6061
(703) 893-8614 (TDD)

Services: This center collects and distributes information on children with disabilities. It connects people with other people who can provide a needed service and maintains a data base of related information.

National Support Center for Persons with Disabilities
P.O. Box 2150
Atlanta, GA 30055
(800) IBM-2133 (Voice)
(800) 284-9482 (TDD)

Services: This center distributes the following directories:

"Resource Guide for Persons with Learning Impairments,"

"Resource Guide for Persons with Mobility Impairments,"

"Resource Guide for Persons with Speech or Language Impairments."

The Orton Dyslexia Society (ODS)
8600 LaSalle Road
Chester Building, Suite 382
Baltimore, MD 21286
(410) 296-0232

Services: The society provides information about dyslexia and provides a referral service for diagnosis and tutoring.

Recordings for the Blind (RFB)
20 Roszel Road
Princeton, NJ 08540
(609) 452-0606
(800) 221-4792

Services: This organization provides taped books for students who cannot read printed materials because of visual problems or specific learning disabilities. An applicant must be identified by a formal evaluation administered within the last three years. Their books range from late elementary school to graduate level and beyond. They are constantly adding new titles.

Stuttering Resource Foundation
123 Oxford Road
New Rochelle, NY 10804
(914) 632-3925
(800) 232-4775

Services: This agency provides information about professionals to contact, support groups, and specific information related to your needs. They maintain a mailing list for disseminating information about new developments.

Appendix D

Related Publications

Anderson, Ruth M., Madeline Miles, and Patricia A. Matheny, editors. *Communicative Evaluation Chart.* Educators Publishing Services, Inc., 1963.

Ayres, A. Jean. *Sensory Integration and the Child.* Western Psychological Services, Los Angeles, CA, 1981.

Bamforth, Amy, and Gay Farley. "Putting the Special Needs Service Puzzle Together." *Child Care News,* vol. 15, no. 5, January/February, 1989.

Barbe, Walter B., Ph.D., and Raymond Swassing, Ed.D. *Teaching Through Modality Strengths: Concepts and Practices.* Zaner-Bloser, Inc..

Conture, Edward G., Ph.D., and Jane Fraser, editors. *Stuttering and Your Child: Questions and Answers.* Speech Foundation of America, 1989.

Directory of National Information Sources on Disabilities. U.S. Department of Education, Office of Special Education and Rehabilitative Services, Washington, DC 20202.

Downey, John A., and Niels L. Low, editors. *The Child with Disabling Illness: Principles of Rehabilitation*. Raven Press, NY, 1982—Chapter 7, "Attention Deficit Disorder, Hyperactivity and Learning Disability: The Minimal Brain Dysfunction Syndrome," by Edward J. Hart and Sidney Carter.

Dumtschin, Joyce Ury. "Recognize Language Development and Delay in Early Childhood." *Young Children,* March, 1988, pp. 16–24.

Exceptional Parents' Annual Directory of National Organizations. 1170 Commonwealth Avenue, Boston, MA 02134, 1990-91.

Freeman, Elsie, M.D. "A Description of Youngsters with Organization/Output Difficulties or Attention Deficit Disorder (ADD)."

Friedman, Jenny. "Helping Your Learning Disabled Child." *Parents,* December, 1989, pp. 106–112.

Gesell Institute of Human Development. Preschool Test for Evaluating Motor, Adaptive, Language and Personal-Social Behavior in Children Ages 2½–6. 1979.

Kuncaitis, Arunas, Ed.D. "Attention Deficit Disorder without Hyperactivity: An Overlooked Diagnosis." *Insights,* vol. 1, no. 2, July, 1990.

Mangrum, Charles T. II, Ed.D. and Stephen S. Strichart, Ph.D. *Colleges with Programs for Learning-Disabled Students.* Peterson's Guides, Princeton, NJ, 1992.

McCall, Robert B., Ph.D. "A Parent's Guide to Learning and School Problems." Boys Town Communication & Public Service Division, Father Flanagan's Boys Home, Boys Town, NE 68010.

McMillan, Joann, OTAS. "Play Is Child's Work," A Home Activity Guide for Parents and their Children. AtlanticCare OT Department.

Receptive-Expressive Emergent Language Scale-Bzoch-League Zimmerman Preschool Language Scale-Zimmer et al. 1979.

Rubin, Nancy. "The Truth about ADHD." *Parents,* February, 1989, pp. 111–112, 193-197.

Sattler, Jerome M. *Assessment of Children.* San Diego State University, 1988.

Silver, Larry B., M.D. *The Misunderstood Child. A Guide for Parents of Learning Disabled Children.* New York, McGraw-Hill, 1984.

Smit, Ann Bosma, Linda Hand, J. Joseph Freilinger, John E. Bernthal, and Ann Bird. "The Iowa Articulation Norms Project and Its Nebraska Replication." American Speech-Language-Hearing Association, *Journal of Speech and Hearing Disorders,* vol. 55, November, 1990, pp. 779–798.

Their World. A publication of the National Center for Learning Disabilities, 99 Park Avenue, New York, NY 10016, 1992.

Tuttle, Cheryl Gerson, and Penny Paquette. *Thinking Games to Play with Your Child.* Lowell House, Los Angeles, CA, 1991.

Understanding Learning Disabilities, A Parent Guide and Workbook. The Learning Disabilities Council, Richmond, VA, 1991.

Index